Joseph F. Sica

Forgiveness

ONE STEP
at a TIME

To my sister and my best friend,
Ann M. Straneva!
Your forgiving spirit is contagious!

To
The Honorable Michael and Linda Barrasse, M.D.
Brian J. Cali
Salvatore and Susan Cognetti, Jr.
Louis and Betty Ann DeNaples
Bruce and Cindy Schoenberg
For their loyalty, honor, and integrity!

Second printing 2010

TWENTY-THIRD PUBLICATIONS
A Division of Bayard
One Montauk Avenue, Suite 200
New London, CT 06320
(860) 437-3012 or (800) 321-0411
www.23rdpublications.com

ISBN 978-1-58595-762-0
Library of Congress Catalog Card Number: 2009936618
Printed in the U.S.A.

Published in Canada by Novalis

Publishing Office
10 Lower Spadina Avenue, Suite 400
Toronto, Ontario, Canada
M5V 2Z2

Head Office
4475 Frontenac Street
Montréal, Québec, Canada
H2H 2S2

www.novalis.ca
ISBN 978-2-89646-214-8

Cataloguing in Publication is available from Library and Archives Canada.

We acknowledge the financial support of the Government of Canada through
the Book Publishing Industry Development Program (BPIDP) for our publishing activities.

CONTENTS

❧ ACKNOWLEDGMENTS ❧

No one walks the journey of life alone and neither do I. I have so many people to thank.

First I want to offer special appreciation and gratitude to my editor, Gwen Costello, for her talent and patience. The publication of this book would not have been possible without Gwen's dedicated efforts. She read my drafts, understood my message, and helped me to say what I wanted to say. The detailed attention and care she has given my words is only outdone by the care she offers every person who crosses her path.

Thank you, Dan Smart of Twenty-Third Publications for your outstanding help. Dan, I'm grateful for your inspiration and motivation in bringing this book to reality. You will never know this side of heaven how much I appreciate you for giving me the dream to write about forgiveness. Without you, this book would just have remained a dream.

My warm and special thanks to Father Michael Piccola and Father David Betts, who inspire me with their strong convictions, unwavering values, passionate love for Jesus Christ, and a deep appreciation for our rich Catholic tradition.

Thank you to the staff, patients, and their families at Mercy Hospital. Most of the stories in this book are taken from their heartfelt sharing. Many of the forgiveness concepts I have learned, I learned directly from listening to them. I hope their voices become like a chorus for taking forgiveness seriously. Their love, honesty, and vulnerability have inspired me to be a better and more forgiving person.

Thank you to my brother priests of the Diocese of Scranton who continue to offer me solid advice and words of encouragement.

So many others have contributed to my life and my ministry with their care and concern, and just knowing you are out there is a lifetime's treasure. Thank you!

I also need to thank two wonderful people who have changed me completely, Joseph and Elveria Sica, Jr., my father and mother. They taught me humility and how to value the lives, thoughts, and expressions of others and how to care for and understand their needs. Though both have died, not a day goes by without me thinking of them and missing them. They still live in my heart.

And lastly to my sister Ann Straneva who is my best friend. She has stood by me and had to listen to me as I read and re-read each and every chapter. She gave me a quiet space to write, cooked me dinner while I was working, brought me a soda when I needed a break, and read over the book for me. She has been the inspiration that has driven me onwards. She has kept me focused.

I have poured my heart and soul into these pages, so now I pray that my words touch the hearts and souls of all who read them.

"They are waiting on the shingle—will you come and join the dance? Will you, won't you, will you, won't you, will you join the dance?"

❧ LEWIS CARROLL, *ALICE IN WONDERLAND*

Forgiveness
One Step at a Time

❧ INTRODUCTION ❧

Betsy was devastated when her husband left her for another woman. Like many who have been betrayed, she was angry, resentful, and bitter. Despite his efforts to maintain their friendship, Betsy refused his calls and denied his request for unlimited visitations with their children.

I suggested to Betsy that she forgive her husband for his actions and forgive herself for any part she may have played in their break-up. She was, in a word, stunned by this suggestion. "Forgive him!" she cried. "Are you crazy? I'd die first! I want to get *even*! I want him to hurt like I hurt!" As she spoke, her face took on a frightening look. Clearly, she was consumed with revenge as she bleated, one last time, "How can you tell me to forgive him?"

I answered her, "I'm not asking you to forgive him because what he did was acceptable. It wasn't; it was mean and selfish. Instead, I'm asking you to forgive because he doesn't deserve the power to live in your head and turn you into a bitter, angry woman. I'd like to see him out of your life emotionally as completely as he is out of it physically, but by being so angry and vengeful you keep holding on to him. You're not hurting him by holding on to your resentment; you're hurting yourself."

Skip the Revenge

There is no such thing as true revenge. It simply does not exist. You can hurt someone even worse than they hurt you, yet it will never "even the score." There is a saying, "Acid does more damage to the vessel it is stored in than to what it is poured on."

For proof of this truism, just look at poor Betsy. Who was getting burned by the venom she kept spewing and, worse, that churned inside? Clearly, she was. Her ex-husband had gone his merry way and was living his life while Betsy stayed in neutral, idling with hate; he didn't deserve the power that she had given him.

Her acceptance of the "victim" role had turned her into a righteous, vindictive, unhappy, and, frankly, unpleasant woman. Those who reached out to help her often found themselves in her warpath, unwitting objects of the diatribes she clearly wished to lob at her ex instead. She kept reliving the hurt, and telling the story, over and over again. Unfortunately, Betsy's behavior is typical of many people who find that forgiveness is the most misunderstood quality in life—often dismissing it as ridiculous, foolish, or both.

I must confess that my advice to Betsy was both personal, as her friend, and professional, as her spiritual counselor. After all, forgiveness runs through the teaching of Jesus as an essential trait on our journey to authentic discipleship. Jesus speaks in a very specific manner about forgiveness. Consider it with me. In the Lord's Prayer we pray: "Forgive us our trespasses as we forgive those who trespass against us."

And in verse 14 of Matthew 6 we read: "For if you forgive others when they sin against you, your Father will also forgive you." In Mark 11:26, Jesus is clear and precise: "And when you stand to pray, if you hold anything against anyone, forgive them, so that your Father in heaven may forgive your sins." And Jesus on the cross having had the very worst done to him prays: "Father forgive them…"

With Jesus, there is no room for unfinished business. In Matthew 5 verse 21, we are told: "…if you are offering your gift at the altar and there remember that someone has something against you, leave your gift there in front of the altar. First go and be reconciled; then come and offer your gift." And in Luke

6 verse 37: "Forgive and you will be forgiven." Make no bones about it, Jesus is serious when it comes to forgiveness!

Nothing is watered down for Jesus and there are no loopholes. When Peter asks Jesus "How many times should I forgive someone? Seven?" The answer given by Jesus is "Seventy times seven," followed by drawing us a picture with the parable of the ungrateful servant (Matthew 18:21–35). Pretty strong words from our gentle and peaceful Lord, am I right? Such is the wisdom we can take away from his message of forgiveness.

Talk is Cheap, Action Divine

It's easy to talk about how important forgiveness is, but much tougher to actually do it in real life. Real-deal followers take Jesus seriously when it comes to forgiveness. Real-deal followers know forgiveness is not a superficial event; they also know it isn't as cut-and-dried as ignoring "unforgivable" behavior.

Forgiveness—*true* forgiveness—isn't about approving damaging behavior or forgetting about what was said or done. These actions always remain a part of our lives; just ask Betsy! Instead, forgiveness is about making what is tragically broken right again.

Forgiveness is about a deep healing, a thorough repair of broken relationships, a removal of the poison that destroys love and harmony, a restoration of wholeness and open trust. It's the only way to reshape our relationships from the straight line of anger and vindictiveness to the curve of connection.

Few of us escape the natural, almost primal urge for revenge. Every single one of us has been hurt by someone else. It may have been a parent who didn't protect us, a sibling who abused us, a friend who betrayed us, a spouse who took us for granted, a pastor who should have been more attentive, a committee member who opposed us, or hundreds of other possibilities that make life's many relationships seem more like land mines of opportunity, ripe for betrayal. Action can be as hurtful as inaction, and vice versa; it may have been something that somebody should have done but didn't. It may be something that took place over many years. It may be something that happened in a moment.

When we hurt, we naturally want to strike back. We're only human, after all. It's in our nature to seek revenge. We think we need an eye for an eye and a tooth for a tooth. Thanks to the "get even" attitude of our modern society, or simply the blaze and haze that accompanies the act of betrayal, we often lose perspective.

Regardless, when someone wrongs us, we want them to pay. When someone makes us suffer, we want them to know the same (or greater) kind of suffering. We want justice. We want the other person to know the pain they inflicted, publicly if possible—privately at bare minimum. And if we can't have justice in some physical way that validates our rage, we vow we'll never have a relationship with that person again. The problem: we don't know when to stop. We want the scales tipped in our favor regardless of the cost, the duration, or the expiration date.

Why is it that happiness is so fleeting and revenge so permanent? Ask people when the last time somebody helped them, complimented, or befriended them was, and you can practically hear crickets chirping as you await a reply. But ask someone when they were last wronged, insulted, cut off in traffic, or betrayed, even ten or twenty years ago, and they remember every detail.

Although we've often spent years developing a relationship, we can still allow a single harsh statement or a thoughtless act to destroy everything we feel for that person. There seem to be no "gray areas" when it comes to revenge; if you're not with us, you're against us. We forget the good, and rationalize bitter, vindictive scenarios that weaken our personality, our happiness, our hope, and our spirit.

But it doesn't have to be this way. When someone we trusted hurts us badly, we *do* have choices:

1. Go our separate ways. Never talk again.
2. Live with accusation, blame, and anger.
3. Bear grudges, nurse hate, or seek revenge.
4. Pretend everything is fine. Bury our feelings.
5. Keep chewing on that hurt. Never let it heal.
6. Talk it through face-to-face with the person and forgive.

Unfortunately, we too often choose to hold a grudge rather than confronting and forgiving. We keep dipping into our store of grievances to find yet another weapon to lob at our opponent:

1. "And another thing…"
2. "You always…"
3. "You never…"
4. "You did the same thing last week…"
5. "I've never forgotten how you…"

Ten Simple Steps

The choice is up to you, of course. No one can tell you the proper time, or even way, to forgive. As for myself, I can only point out the harm that refusing to forgive can cause, as I've seen it played out time and time again with parishioners or patients who refuse to let go of that hurt—long after the grievance has occurred.

It is said that grief has many stages and that there's a natural progression in the grieving process. I propose that forgiveness is much the same. For me, in fact, forgiveness is a well-choreographed dance with ten distinctive steps.

1. Ruined: handling injury
2. Retreat: getting stuck
3. Revenge: wanting payback
4. Rehearse: telling everybody
5. Rethink: waking up
6. Respond: loving confrontation
7. Reminder: setting boundaries
8. Repair: patching up
9. Reward: reaping benefits
10. Release: moving on

Dance Like No One's Watching

Dance is the perfect metaphor to describe forgiveness, since hurts are inevitable in life's ever-changing tempo. Dancing involves being in sync with our hurts, being attuned to our needs and emotional rhythm. With each dance step we gain a new perspective, restoring a bit more of what we lost. Each step leads to greater wisdom and understanding of forgiveness as a worthwhile and healthy way of life.

I know that even as I write these words urging you to forgive, there may be a situation or person that immediately pops into your mind and begins to make your stomach churn. In the course of my ministry, I've seen hundreds of people who "fall out of step" with their dance of forgiveness and continue to harbor past hurts well beyond a hurtful act's "expiration date." They stay tied up in knots, out of sync with happiness or hope, because they simply refuse to forgive. As a result they are handcuffed, emotionally if not physically, to their offender. Like Marley's ghost, they follow them through eternity, always a step behind because they refuse to move forward. As a result, they give the offender rent-free space in their heads and hearts. In a very real way, the revenge they seek is like being betrayed all over again, although the offender may be unaware or uncaring about their inability to forgive.

True forgiveness, of course, is always more than a technique or formula. It's a matter of the heart and of what one truly believes is at the very center of reality. Forgiveness is a way of releasing oneself from the pain experienced at the hands of others in order to experience a softer, kinder, and easier way of life.

Break Your Addiction

Forgive the other person for once; do this one thing for yourself. Resentment and revenge are heavy loads to carry. We have to work to change these feelings. In many ways, we are like addicts and revenge is our drug of choice. We may even want to forgive, but it's much more comfortable for our wired brains to fall back into revenge mode, regardless of the consequences to our personal and professional lives.

Only forgiveness can set us free and "break" our revenge addiction. And, much like recovery from any other addiction, forgiveness is a journey and a choice. As we have seen, when we continue to cling to the pain we associate with revenge, we're truly only damaging ourselves.

Can we ever move on? I believe we can—when we take Jesus seriously about forgiveness.

Perhaps one day Betsy will realize that she did her best in that relationship, and that her husband truly believed that he did his best as well. Certainly we don't condone intentional, hurtful behavior, but we do encourage forgiveness once a hurtful act has been committed, regardless of the circumstance. By letting go, by forgiving, Betsy can finally release the negative emotion that has gripped her so tightly and be free to move forward and love again.

And so I offer these ten easy-to-follow forgiveness dance steps and I have choreographed them to connect with the message of Jesus. Each dance step to forgiveness includes: something to learn (path); something to consider (ponder); something to do (practice); and something to say (prayer).

So, shall we dance?

Ruined

Handling Injury

"Love your enemies, bless those who curse you, do good to those who hate you, and pray for those who spitefully use you and persecute you."

— MATTHEW 5:44

Life is not risk- or pain-free. No one gets through it without being hurt by another person. Some people, I've found, seem to make a habit of hurting others. Perhaps they spoke an unkind word or passed a thoughtless remark; maybe they joined in the gossip; they cheated in a business deal; they were inattentive as parents; they were unappreciative children; they disappointed in a time of crisis; they broke their vows. Regardless, the pain of betrayal is the same. We feel violated, having to deal with an injury caused by someone else for no deserving reason.

We'll all be betrayed, hurt, and wronged many times over in this life. We'll all have volumes of injuries and bruises to store in our "warehouses." To forgive, to set ourselves free of accumulated pain and betrayal, we must first recognize that we are injured and then begin to heal.

Something to Learn (Path)

"I feel like roadkill on the highway of love," said Marty philosophically as he sat in my office one day, "and I ain't gonna be that for nobody!" It was Susan's series of affairs that finally led to their divorce. She'd always leave the house with a new explanation, but Marty knew she was lying.

"She kept promising me she would stop, but she didn't," he explained. "All I have left is this emptiness inside and a broken heart. It's the worst feeling in the world to be dumped for another person." His face was red, his teeth were clenched, and the veins in his forehead threatened to pop. "I'll get even with Susan if it's the last thing I do!"

Marty is dancing our first step: *Ruined.*

We've All Danced This Step

As noted, because we live in an imperfect world, we've all been hurt. Our deepest hurts have come from other people. Believe it or not, relationships are the greatest source of stress in our lives. Not jobs, not money, not housing, food, clothing, or commerce. Who we relate with, and who relates back, can make life worth living—or fill us with revenge. Our relationships can also be our greatest blessing and our greatest joy. But people do hurt us, sometimes intentionally, sometimes unintentionally, sometimes accidentally, and sometimes on purpose.

For some, being betrayed by a relationship means being abused physically, emotionally, or verbally as a child, being pushed around or put down, beaten up, or berated. "You'll never amount to anything!" "You're not smart enough, pretty enough, or good enough." Unfortunately, such betrayals don't have an expiration date; they stretch on and on into other areas of life long after they have occurred. Many carry these wounds well into adulthood and throughout the rest of their lives, always wondering if those angry words and insults were true and deserved; always doubting themselves.

For others betrayal means being injured by a spouse who walks out one day, leaving only a note ("I'm out of here. Don't even try to contact me"), three young children to raise, and a mountain of unpaid bills. Or it could be a spouse who sticks around, but constantly takes the other for granted and betrays emotional trust; in short, a person who sucks the joy out of life through negative, controlling, selfish, and hypocritical behavior.

Families account for some of the most joyous and disappointing relationships. Fairness of the give-and-take balance develops a sense of trust between family members. Trustworthiness builds assurances that one's needs will be met without manipulation or threats of retaliation. Often that trustworthiness breaks down because someone feels betrayed.

Unfortunately, hurts in families can last for years, cutting both wide and deep, and can even be passed down through generations. We've all heard these comments: "I haven't talked to my sister since I left home at eighteen," or "No one associates with Uncle Joe after he ran Dad's business into the ground twenty-three years ago."

Blaming God

Friends, family, colleagues, neighbors: who is left to cause us hurt in this life? Well some believe even God causes injury. When "God" disappoints us, we become upset and carry a grudge. For many people, in fact, this becomes the ultimate betrayal. When I encounter people with a grudge against God, almost universally it wasn't a prolonged series of events that caused so much pain, but usually one single tragic incident.

A young couple I know has been carrying a grudge against God for nearly ten years. Their beautiful five-year-old daughter died shortly after being stricken with a brain tumor. They grew bitter. They didn't quit going to church; they still went through all the motions. But they no longer believed in prayer. They're afraid to disown God; afraid to call God a liar or unfaithful. But there is no question about their deep-seated grudge and the wedge it has caused between themselves and their spiritual life. They've said it on several occasions, "We'll never forgive God for taking away our only child."

In our hospital cafeteria one day I heard two men talking.

One asked, "Have you been to church lately?"

The other one replied, "No, not since my father died. God knew how much I loved my father! And I haven't been back to church since."

Clearly this man's pain is evident and he was very quick to assign the blame. What can be done to reverse the tide, heal the pain, and dissolve the wedge between resentment and forgiveness? Given the immense hurt inflicted on us, it's hardly surprising if we struggle with forgiveness in this early dance step.

Revenge Points Back

We find forgiveness hard to do and, if accomplished, even harder to sustain; so we avoid it at all costs. We latch onto the popular stance of holding others forever accountable. We somehow believe that if we stamp out the offender (who, of course, deserves to be eliminated or at least "taught a lesson") we'll feel good and our personal world will be a safe and happy place.

Our culture encourages us. Revenge is for the strong, the vital, the honorable, the American; forgiveness, on the other hand, is for wimps. Revenge is "only right," "an eye for an eye," and all that implies. But what is revenge if not the vain attempt to right a wrong that can't be taken back, disavow words that can't be unspoken, or erase a memory that is indelible? Revenge is our attempt to go back in time, to right what was wrong, to "put it all back together again."

In many ways we can see revenge as the gun in our hand, ready to fire, only this gun only points in one direction; straight back at our faces! We only hurt ourselves with vengeful thoughts, vengeful acts, and vengeful obsessions. Grudges become frozen in time and hatchets are never buried. The hurt we feel is very real, very deep, and sometimes very private. Most people, even those closest to us, don't understand the depth of the hurts we carry as a result of the emotional injuries we have experienced. We assume that we must be strong and not show weakness; not let the person who hurt us, or even others who are close to us, know how damaged, broken, and injured we feel. Above all, we must not give in and forgive. The message of Jesus is counter to all this. He says to forgive seven times seventy, no matter the offense, and even from the cross he cried, "Father, forgive them, they don't know what they're doing." That is *real* strength.

Why Is This Happening?

Perhaps the worst part about betrayal is that we didn't invite, solicit, or deserve what was done to us. It simply happened. "Why is this happening to ME?" we ask, finding our only answer to be more pain, suffering, and confusion. It takes some time to process the actual meaning of our hurt and its long-term effects. Imagine finding out that your spouse has been having an affair. In our opening anecdote, Marty had long suspected his wife, Susan, of infidelity but, in most cases, as in his, we simply can't believe it.

Here is the person we chose to be with forever, 'til death do us part; here is our soulmate, whom we swore an oath to love, honor, and cherish—and this person betrayed us? Shock isn't the word for how we feel. Worse still, we may not want to accept the facts and choose not to believe it for some period of time. As a result we live in limbo, halfway between the life we had and the life we should be living. Unable to go back, unable to move forward, we are literally stuck to dwell in our pain and grief.

When injury happens to us, our first reaction is disbelief. We express our disbelief in various ways: "I can't believe it happened." "I just can't get over it"; "It happened out of the blue"; "I was just stunned by it"; "I'm completely taken aback by…" "It's the worst thing that could have happened to me." These are natural responses. We feel numb during this time and can hardly express any feelings, other than simply repeating, parrot-like, the above phrases. The process works subtly, giving us moments away from our pain and allowing us to pace our feelings of hurt. It's nature's way of letting in only as much as we can handle; consider this period life's version of your car's shock-absorbers.

Since we often don't know how to cope with our hurts, our response is to turn to things that usually mess us up and cause more problems in our lives. We drink too much, smoke too much, eat too much, sleep too much, spend too much to bury our pain. These are temporary stop-gap measures that only put us in more pain when the bill comes due: the hangover the next morning or the extra weight that causes us to feel even more insecure.

The only way to break out of limbo, to move forward, is to stop this cycle of avoidance. This is a dance, remember, and what dance do you know where you just stand still? None. To keep dancing toward forgiveness, you need to avoid two poor moves: denial and hiding. And if you insist on keeping these in your repertoire—welcome to misery.

Denial: Never Happened

I don't know about you, but there have been times in my life when others hurt me and I pretended my hurt didn't exist. I often ignored the elephant sitting across the table from me! I would sit under its weight and pretend it was light as a feather. In truth, I was hoping it would go away before I had to actively take stock and do something about it. Isn't this human nature?

Obviously the pain was real, the betrayal was an actual event, and the offender was someone close to me, but for the sake of survival it was easier to put on a perfect smile and pretend "it" wasn't happening. "She hurt me?" I might ask as if surprised. "Who, me? No way; her comment rolled right off my back. I didn't give it a second thought."

Then I would bite the bullet. Suck it up. Suffer in silence. Hope it will go away. Flat out denial; "Nothing happened," sprinkled with minimizing; "It was no big deal. She didn't hurt me that badly"; and procrastination; "I'll deal with this, just as soon as...." So, we avoid it, postpone it, play it down, and do nothing about it. We sweep it under the carpet and just put it off. But where do you think it goes? Does it disappear, never to be seen again? Or does it snowball while we're not looking, growing bigger and bigger until it's simply too big to avoid any longer? I think you know the answer.

A short period of denial may be beneficial, providing us with time to adjust to our hurt. In fact, this phase can be part of the healing process; being in denial temporarily helps us to cope with the hurt we want to ignore. It gives our mind the opportunity to unconsciously absorb shocking or distressing information at a pace that won't send us into a tailspin.

When denial persists, however, and prevents us from dealing with our pain, it becomes harmful. It's like the weekend warrior who sprains his ankle on Saturday and tries to be "tough" about it. If he waits a little while to watch and see if the swelling goes down on its own, he's only being prudent. But if he waits until the middle of the week when the ankle is simply too painful to walk on, prudence has turned into carelessness.

Certainly, running to the ER every time we stub our toe is counterproductive, but waiting too long to address a real injury can mean it's too late for complete healing. Eventually, we simply can't ignore it any longer.

I'm not saying it's naïve or irresponsible to slip into denial when we are hurt, but when we use denial as a way to cope with and solve our hurts, we are strapping on inner tubes to survive tidal waves! Sure, in the beginning of the storm, we can blissfully float through the situation, letting the inner tubes of denial keep us afloat. But eventually, our hurts will only get worse, flooding our heads with feelings we'll find hard to shake loose. Our inner tubes will form holes and, before we know it, we'll begin to sink from our own denial. If you have ever felt like you were drowning or sinking, this is a sign that denial is slipping out of control. Choosing to live with denial isn't coping; it's copping out. It's perpetually dancing the same routine over and over again and *never getting anywhere.*

Hiding: Nothing's Wrong

We've all got plenty of hurts to go around: a lost friendship; a bitter, painful breakup; someone we love, but who doesn't love us; a job we didn't get; a promotion we deserved but missed out on because we were too young, too old, or too in between; a loved one who has died; a violation; a betrayal; a rejection; a nasty fight. Unless we are born with rhinoceros skin, these things hurt us. Rather than deal with our hurts out loud, however, too often we keep them all to ourselves; we hide from the truth.

We say, "Who could I tell anyway? Who would listen? My friends are so busy with their own lives. Everyone has problems, why bother them with mine?" We wear a mask and camouflage them. We keep them all inside, where no one else can see them, hiding behind a smiling exterior.

Have you ever seen the episode of *The Andy Griffith Show* where Andy, Barney, Opie, and friends are having a hootin', hollerin' time enjoying the Christmas holidays at Mayberry's police headquarters? Unlike most jails, this one comes complete with a Christmas tree, plenty of presents, music, good food, and great friends.

Department store owner Ben Weaver wants in on the fun—but he's too cranky and isolated to admit that he's alone for the holidays. Instead of simply asking to join in, he tries to get arrested. From loitering to littering, he's proof positive that "you can't even get arrested in this town." Finally, Andy realizes that Ben is all alone and simply wants to belong, so he "arrests" him on Christmas Eve. If only Ben would have opened up to America's nicest sheriff, the incarceration wouldn't have shown up on his permanent record!

How often are we like old Ben, too full of pride or hurt or isolation to admit that we're hurting, admit that we're in pain, and seek the help and companionship we need? Unfortunately, most people aren't as sensitive as the fictional Andy Griffith and only catch on when we yell and scream and shout.

Our hurts run very deep and we don't realize that all of our accumulated hurts influence everything we do. We wear nice clothes and have a pleasant smile, but the reality is we've been hurt very deeply and simply aren't the same as we were before it happened. Sometimes we play a game called "Is something wrong?" We always answer, "No, nothing's wrong."

We try to hide our hurts by eating or drinking too much, or by watching too much TV. Sometimes we distract ourselves in positive ways through exercise, creating things, learning new hobbies. Either way, however, denial is denial and the result is the same: We hide our hurts, don't express them, and thus do not heal them.

The hurt doesn't just go away. In fact, our pain is very, very good at lurking, loitering, and hiding. It can recede into the dark corners of the soul and cloak itself in every beat of our heart. A friend of mine had an Easter egg hunt and she could have sworn she dyed and hid three dozen eggs, only the kids came back with just 35! Where did that last egg go? Only too late she realized she had hidden it in the den. By then the egg had spoiled and created a nasty smell that took weeks to air out. Hurt is like that; we can hide our pain so well, and try to forget about it, until it's too late.

Everyone has been hurt. It's different for each, yes, but *everyone* has been hurt. You're not alone. You're not even the only one with the hurt you've got. You may think you are. You may think you're the only one in the world who has suffered this way. But there are others that have the same hurt you do.

Our hurts are legitimate. It is silly to pretend that someone didn't hurt us when, in fact, they did. Even if it was unintentional, pretending it didn't hurt is being dishonest with ourselves, which only compounds the original hurt. After all, if we can't be honest with ourselves, who is left to turn to? We know that it really did hurt, and when we deny that this particular pain exists, we waste our time trying to convince ourselves otherwise.

We don't heal ourselves by denial or hiding; we only delay the inevitable—more pain. To heal our hurts, we have to reconnect with them. We have to bring them out of the closet, attic, or basement where we stashed them and into the living room of our lives.

By coming out from under the burden of silence and acknowledging the hurt and brokenness from our injuries, we experience freedom. We are finally able to let go of the masks we have been hiding behind and let down our guard. Only in the light, with God's help, can we fully feel the hurt, heal it, and deal with it. Only then can we be truly healed, and only then can we be freed from the pain that binds us.

Own It: It's Mine

For us to receive the healing of emotional hurts, we must first own that we are hurting. Jesus tells us in Matthew 9:12: "Those who are well have no need of a physician, but those who are sick do." These is no shame in feeling pain, and there's no time limit on how long you can hurt. But the sooner you admit you need help, the sooner you can get it.

Many of us prefer instead to dance out of step with "denying" and "hiding" as our partners. It's time to learn two new moves and take ownership of them: acknowledge and agreement.

Joyce's Dance Move

Joyce literally collapsed after reading the e-mail that revealed Peter's affair with his old college girlfriend. "I couldn't breathe," she confessed. "I felt light-headed, and I think my heart actually stopped for a moment. That e-mail described in excruciating detail my husband's real-life encounter with his cyber lover. I trusted him completely," she said. "I never imagined he would betray me. How could I have been so stupid?"

And the worst part is that Peter admitted the affair wasn't even necessary in the first place; it was a mistaken attempt on his part to find something he thought was missing in their existing relationship.

What can we take away from this hurtful betrayal? First and foremost, Joyce has been hurt; deeply hurt. No one understands the depth of pain an unfaithful spouse brings to a tender heart more than one who has been through it.

When Joyce came to see me, she said, "I want to get my marriage back on track. Peter's a good person. He had many admirable qualities before our marriage took a turn for the worse, and I keep reminding myself that the affair doesn't erase those qualities. I don't want to have that cold yuck feeling in my soul every time I think of Peter. So I can't allow anger, bitterness, and criticism to fill my marriage. I want to get this behind us."

Prior to getting their marriage back on track, Joyce had already chosen to forgive and move forward. Did she have any other choice? After all, they can't return to the marriage they once had. No matter what they say and do from this point forward, those two people are gone forever. But they can, in time, and with lots of work, build a new, stronger marriage. Through forgiveness and understanding, Peter and Joyce are saying: "We believe in our marriage. We want our marriage to keep on going."

I was impressed with the way Joyce handled Peter's affair. She didn't throw her hands up and walk away from it all. She didn't bury her head in the sand and deny Peter's e-mails were real. She didn't go on with life as usual and normal either. She was hurt. She slowed down and took the time she needed to "own" her hurt.

Then she expressed it to Peter. She brought her hurt out in the open and made a decision to move forward. She didn't dance the ten steps to forgiveness by making Peter grovel for it. She didn't use the affair as emotional blackmail or hold it over Peter's head. Instead, Joyce owned what happened and made a conscious decision to start fresh by leaving the past in the past through forgiveness.

Joyce was seriously injured, but she didn't choose denial or hiding. Even though she didn't create the situation, she knew she had to be a part of the solution if she was ever to reconcile her marriage. This is an effective dance move for us when we've been hurt: acknowledge and own it.

Most don't move as quickly as Joyce did; they dance at their own pace. People dance the steps to forgiveness in a variety of ways, from efforts that seem like two steps forward and one step back or all at once. Some move quickly and others move slowly, each individual dances to his or her own pace.

David's Dance Move

On the other side of the emotional spectrum, we have David's story. David came to see me and he shared how he has spent a good deal of his life angry. In fact, after one terribly horrific breakup, he was angry for more than thirteen years! Not surprisingly, this breakup was the result of a betrayal. The grudge was embedded. Lack of owning his hurt turned him into one angry, grudge-holding person. Despite not liking these feelings, David carried them around all this time. This major disappointment knocked the wind out of his sails. It was a blow that left him feeling numb—morning, noon, and night. It was always on his mind and he couldn't accept what Patricia had done. Well-meaning friends told him to "snap out of it," but he didn't.

More accurately, David *couldn't*.

David had trouble sleeping and regularly dreamed that Patricia came back, begging for forgiveness, and, "like an idiot," he told me, he'd forgive her, only to have it happen again. He'd wake up, incredibly depressed and angry. He said it was just as if the whole betrayal had happened all over again. He had effectively vacuum-sealed the break-up. By keeping the hurt alive, it was always fresh and new.

By coming to see me, David was finally confessing to the hurt; he was effectively "owning" it. Now he could address it. David told me, "I still have a long road ahead to completely let go of what happened and forgive Patty, but I have finally come to the place in my life where I am able to speak her name without venom and choking back tears."

Since David has owned and acknowledged Patricia's betrayal and his hurt, his moments of anger and unhappiness are lessening. Perhaps one day they will disappear altogether. David is finally dancing the first step toward forgiveness.

Yes! Acknowledge it!

Denial is like trying to dance the tango with our shoelaces tied together. We simply cannot dance all the way to forgiveness without acknowledging what was done to us. That means accepting it. For example, if I was badly abused as a child, I cannot reach a point of forgiveness unless I reach a point where I can first acknowledge the abuse. This may seem straightforward to the rest of us, but many adults who were abused as children remain protective of their parents, minimizing what was done to them ("It wasn't so bad"), or even blaming themselves ("I was bad and deserved what I got"). To forgive, we must first face the reality of what was done to us.

As tough as it is to believe, acceptance is the one essential requirement needed to start healing our hurts. Of course, it seems a radical concept to consider accepting the very hurt that is making us miserable. Why not just keep it buried inside a little while longer? But we know for a fact that turning our back on the hurt or putting on a happy-face mask and trying to pretend everything is all right doesn't work in the long run.

The great psychologist Carl Jung stated, "We can't change anything until we accept it." Our acceptance of the injury done to us and the hurt we are experiencing allows us to begin dancing toward forgiveness.

Rachel shared with me her hurt in the form of rejection and disappointment when her boss promised her a promotion. When the time came to award it, her rival at work was given the job instead. She said, "I was hurt. Extremely angry. Totally disappointed. For me, acceptance took some time. It took me many months to give myself permission to forgive my boss. What worked for me was to stop and breathe. Then to ask myself how things would be different if I were to just accept that this is the way it is. Once I did, I was able to make better decisions about my employment, how I wanted to respond to my boss and coworker, and where I wanted to go from here."

It helped in this case that Rachel was very results-oriented. Before acting out, perhaps even irrationally, she stopped and asked herself, "What would the result of my actions be?" Then she could take a breath and move forward in a way that built bridges instead of burning them.

I love the story that tells of an old man who accidentally fell into the river rapids. The man was swept up by the river into a high and dangerous waterfall. Onlookers feared for his life. Miraculously, he came out alive and unharmed downstream at the bottom of the falls. People asked him how he managed to survive.

"I accommodated myself to the water," he told them, "not the water to me. Without thinking, I allowed myself to be shaped by it. Plunging into the swirl, I came out with the swirl. This is how I survived."

I see this inspirational story as suggesting that first we must accept whatever injury and hurts are currently upon us. There is no point in denying it or hiding it or attempting to stop the hurt. We can crawl into bed and curl into a little ball for days on end or we can stop, catch a breath, and accept the hurt.

Accepting the injury done by others is not as difficult as we may think. We only have to accept what is happening in this moment, not in every moment throughout time. It doesn't mean we have to approve of it or like it; quite the contrary. All we have to do is accept it, since that's the way it is. Accept that the present situation is not a happy one for us, and that if there is to be any change, we alone must make it first. Acceptance is taking ownership of our hurts and putting us in the driver's seat of our own recovery.

Be Alert!

When it comes to our cars, preventive maintenance is the $35 oil change that keeps us from having to shell out for the $1,500 new transmission! Why should care along life's roadside be any different? Since all of us have to experience the bitter disappointment of people who hurt us, we need to be on the alert by keeping our eyes open, keeping our guard up, and watching our backs so we are insulated and protected from future damage.

Some hurts involve people who are only peripherally in our lives. In those cases, we choose another path and put the bad experience behind us. But when the experience involves relationships from which we cannot easily walk away—parents who belittle us; lifelong friends who betray us; a "dream" boyfriend or girlfriend who jilts us—we need to be ready to respond when they try it again.

Stephanie told me, "I had to wake up and smell the coffee, and realize my relationship was over. Alan wouldn't commit to the relationship. I caught him cheating several times and he kept hurting me over and over. Each time I would accept his apology, take him back, and continue the relationship, only to get hurt again. I had to own my hurt and accept the end and not cling to the hope that a miracle would happen and things would go back to normal. I started thinking with my head and not my heart. Alan never showed any signs of improvement or maturity, so I had to end the relationship, accept that Alan wouldn't be there for me any more, and keep him out of my life."

Mind you, none of this happened overnight. It took time for Stephanie to stop feeling the hurt in her heart. Getting over the breakup wasn't easy, especially in the first weeks after the "let's just be friends" speech. For awhile, in fact, the misery and heartache took over her entire life and made it practically unlivable. She gradually and cautiously, with time and patience, danced to forgiveness, so her emotions wouldn't erupt one day in a harmful way.

Stephanie says, "I learned the hard way that I'm not someone's punching bag or someone's doormat."

You Decide

Who among us does not have an injured relationship or two in the rearview mirror littering our personal landscape? Who isn't haunted by some offense from our past? Forgiveness cannot be forced, especially if we've been abused, neglected, or treated cruelly, or have suffered trauma at the hands of others. What they did caused hurt, disrespect, harm, betrayal, violation, cheating, wounding, or destruction.

When teachers show up to a playground fight, their first question is "Who started it?" For those of us who have been pummeled on life's not-so-playful ground, the more urgent and more useful question is, "Who can end it?" The first is a question about the past, and we cannot change the past. But the second is about the present and the future, and these are things we can affect by our own decision.

Owning our hurts doesn't mean we're giving up, but it does mean we can look around and say, "What choices do I have with what has been done to me?" But how we manage the injury done to us after this first step determines whether we become a *bitter person* or a *better person*. Did you notice? The minor difference between bitter and better is the letter "i."

I make the choice.

I choose whether the injury will devastate me or direct me to continue dancing toward forgiveness.

I decide whether to learn new dance moves or repeat the same routine over and over with the same results.

There can be no middle ground to this decision: either we decide to forgive the person who hurt us, or we hold onto bitterness and anger—perhaps indefinitely. We are not ballerinas in a music box, destined to perpetual motion for as long as we exist. Real dancers tire and regroup, rest and refresh, try new dance moves and throw out others. Life—the dance—is in perpetual motion.

Are we?

All of what we've done during the first dance step can be undone if we begin to dwell on the event again and refuse to keep dancing. If we begin to rerun our mind's movie of the injury, we may find ourselves stuck in those two missteps we discussed: denial and hiding.

We go home, sit in a chair or lie in bed, and hurt takes over. After tossing and turning we finally get to sleep and when we wake up, the hurt continues. Why? Because we replay the encounter that hurt us over and over in our heads, adding what we wished we had said or what we could have done differently.

Jeff told me every place he goes, the heated argument he had with Roseanne follows him. Like a shadow stalking him, things unsaid follow him through good times and bad. He said, "I wish I had said what I really wanted to say to Roseanne, but I didn't. Now I could kick myself for holding back."

I hear it all the time in my ministry, whether it's small stuff like a thoughtless comment or being made the brunt of someone's joke, to colossal things like a trusted friend who lied to us and hurt us, or the mother who refuses to let us live our own lives, or the driver who fell asleep and cost us something precious. We each have something or someone to forgive.

No matter how big or how small, the difference begins with "i."

Move the Fence

During World War II, as Allied soldiers fought their way across France, a soldier died during a bloody firefight. After the battle was over, his buddies wanted to find a way to give him a decent burial. The only cemetery in the closest village was a Catholic cemetery so they approached the priest, asking for permission to bury their fallen comrade there.

"Is he Catholic?" asked the priest.

"No, he's Protestant," came the reply.

With great regret, the priest said, "He can't be buried here. This cemetery is reserved for baptized members of the Catholic Church." So the soldiers found a suitable place outside the fence that marked the border of the cemetery. With great sorrow, they buried him and then went back to the war.

Some months later, the soldiers returned to the tiny village, hoping to provide a suitable marker for their friend. To their surprise and consternation, when they came to the burial spot, they couldn't find the grave. Not knowing what else to do, they asked the priest if he knew what had happened. He told them after they had buried their friend, he couldn't sleep at night. So one morning he got up early and *moved the fence* to include the body of the much-loved soldier who had died for his country.

That's what Jesus did for us. He couldn't rest while we're on the wrong side of the fence, allowing our hurts to hurt us and hurt others, by denying and hiding them. Jesus wants so much for us to bring our hurts over to the other side of the fence, to him, so he "moved the fence" so that we could have a place to unload our hurting hearts, where soothing and comfort reside. Let me give you this invitation from Jesus, "Come to me, you who are weary and heavily burdened…and I will give you rest."

His arms are open and waiting.

Some people vow to keep their hurting hearts on their side of the fence where they can safely deny the hurt. An insult received in anger, a slight delivered out of forgetfulness, an unexpected betrayal, or a hurt borne out of a misunderstanding, these hurts roam wild and remain broken. Jesus doesn't deny the reality of our pain, but he does want us to handle it properly.

Denying and hiding can only block out the endless positive possibilities on the other side of the fence. We have to decide to live on the side of the fence where "owning it" resides and forgiveness is possible. The fence has been moved; it is up to us to choose to live within those boundaries he sets, where there's hope and healing—the very heart of the gospel, take it seriously.

The alternative to not dancing on to forgiveness is depicted in C.S. Lewis' book *The Great Divorce*. Lewis pictures hell as a vast, gray city, inhabited only at its outer edges. There are rows and rows of empty houses in the middle. They are empty because everyone who once lived in them quarreled with the neighbors and moved, and quarreled with the new neighbors and moved again, on and on until there was no one left. That, says Lewis, is how hell got so large; people chose distance over dealing with one another and learning to forgive.

Something to Consider (Ponder)

In the movie *Avalon* (1990), Uncle Gabriel stopped talking to his family members for the rest of his life because they started Thanksgiving dinner without him after he was excessively late for the zillionth time.

Who can't relate to either side of this common *faux pas*? If you were waiting for your own Uncle Gabriel for the zillionth time, wouldn't you be tempted to at least nibble on the drumstick sitting there so temptingly on your plate? And if you were Uncle Gabriel, wouldn't you be sorely tempted to feel betrayed by this obvious "slight"?

But forever? What a waste of energy it is to stay angry for decades when with a simple discussion the future can open up like an empty, unbroken road of forgiveness just waiting to be traveled. But don't trust me; rent the movie for yourself and think about something a parishioner named Rhonda once told me: "It only takes a minute to cause hurt but sometimes a lifetime to repair. Be careful with your words and actions."

Something to Do (Practice)

To begin the dance to forgiveness, take a moment and think about a time when someone hurt you. Write down the name of the person (even if he or she is no longer living and you haven't resolved it) who has injured you in some way. Perhaps someone said something thoughtless or hurtful, or someone was neglectful of your feelings or needs; maybe it was a critical parent, a controlling spouse, or a cutthroat colleague.

See this person sitting in front of you, at a distance that feels comfortable to you. If for any reason it is not comfortable for you to invite this person into the sacred space that you have created with your imagination—envision him or her behind a wall of glass or in a room across from yours or see them on the TV screen; be creative and do what feels comfortable. Consider the ways you have been injured. Silently, but clearly, acknowledge this, saying something like "Regarding this person (name them), or situation (name it), I feel hurt." (You will be amazed by how simply admitting you're hurt immediately unburdens you.)

During this first dance step, just stop and bring your hurt out of hiding and own it, acknowledge it, and be aware of it. Next, think about how you felt at the time of the "injury." Feel how hurt or angry or disappointed or resentful you felt. On a scale of 0-10, how strong was your hurt? (Zero being none at all and ten being the strongest you have ever felt anything.)

> *"Give sorrow words."*
>
> SHAKESPEARE

Now pour out your feelings by writing them down. Writing about how we feel and why we are feeling that way can help us to "get it all out," so that eventually we will be able to release the hurt and move on. Here are some guidelines:

- Freely write whatever feelings come to you.

- Write in a private and safe environment.

- Write about the injuries you are thinking about and which you never disclosed, discussed, or resolved.

- Write about what happened without troubling over format. Don't worry about grammar, spelling, or sentence structure.

- Write out how you feel. Don't use big words. Simply write: "I feel _____ and _____." Write out why you feel this way.

- Remember this isn't a time to write down your complaints about the injury. Complaining only makes the injury worse. It's a time to discover *how* and *why* you feel this way. It's critical that you allow yourself to go deep and touch those deepest feelings.

- Take it slowly. The deepest hurts are wrapped up in a lot of confusion and pain, so go easy on yourself and take your time.

I have discovered that to dance to forgiveness and improve how we feel, we must first endure difficult feelings. The more we own our hurt, the more likely we can dance effective steps to move toward healing.

Something to Say (Prayer)

Gracious God, it is your desire that I have good relationships with the people around me—my family, my neighbors and friends, my sisters and brothers in Jesus. And yet, truth be told, there are people in my life with whom my "good" relationships have been broken. I have been hurt; the pain lies deep within my soul. I withhold my love and friendship because of the hurt within.

Lord, I know there are people in my life that I need to forgive. But there are some people I just can't forgive on my own. I need you, O Lord, to give me the words, the desire, the ability to dance through the hurt that leads to forgiveness.

Empower me, O Lord, so that I might embrace the hurt, face my own fears, or in some cases, swallow my own pride, that I might work on forgiving those who have hurt me. If I am going to be whole, O Lord, I must heal the hurt within. In Jesus' name, I pray. Amen.

Retreat

Getting Stuck

*"Then Peter came to him and said, 'Lord, how often
shall my brother sin against me and I forgive him? Up
to seven times?' Jesus said to him, 'I do not say to you
seven times, but up to seventy times seven.'"*

~ MATTHEW 18:21–22

Sometimes hurts are so bad and cut so deep that instead of
going on the offensive we do quite the opposite: We *retreat*.
We may literally retreat, by moving away to avoid running into
the offender. We may retreat physically, by staying inside and
becoming a recluse to avoid confrontation. Or, we may even
retreat spiritually, giving up on love and hope and even God.

Running away from forgiveness is like trying to cut loose from
our shadow. It's impossible. It may go into hiding by nightfall,
but it will always be there when the sun comes up the next
morning. Retreating has the same effect as avoidance or denial.
It keeps us stuck forever in that zone of pain where the grudge
we bear is all we can see, hear, and feel.

Something to Learn (Path)

Anthony can't forgive his sister Louise because she was never there for him; he felt abandoned by her. She has apologized, has tried to make peace, has extended a hand of forgiveness, and wants to be there now for her brother, but he has frozen her out.

Anthony will not allow her into his life and when the family has celebrations or parties (after many beers) Anthony tells everybody, "You can't trust my sister because she will let you down. She wasn't there for me and I almost lost my life."

The family keeps saying, "Not again! Why can't Anthony forgive his sister and move on? Why does he have to keep digging up the past?"

For her part, Louise says, "I guess I just will not bother to go to family get-togethers anymore. It's not worth the embarrassment and the pain to keep living the past over and over, trying to undo something I can't change."

Like Anthony, many of us have been hurt deeply. We're not talking about misunderstandings or petty family disputes; we're talking about deep, ugly, horrible hurts where "forgive and move on" just doesn't cut it.

Stall or Stop?

Forgiveness is a marathon, not a sprint. To forgive too quickly, without processing the pain or coming to terms with our forgiveness, can be as bad as not forgiving at all. Only through the journey to discovery and reconciliation can we come to the destination of our choosing.

Along our journey to having our injuries forgiven and hurts healed, we can easily get detoured, delayed, and distracted from the need to forgive by choosing to "shut out and shut down." When we do this we'll be stuck in "retreat" mode, which will only stall or stop our dance to forgiveness.

There are several possible reasons why an injured person takes the lead when they dance the retreat step.

1. The offense was deeper than they realized.

2. They want to see the offender's behavior change first.

3. They may not have had time to think through what happened.

4. Simply asking forgiveness doesn't erase everything that has happened.

5. Others can't possibly understand how deeply they have been hurt.

6. If they forgive the offender, he or she may strike again and this time cause more severe harm.

Sadly, all of these reasons are valid enough for wanting to retreat. Even more tragic is the fact that retreating doesn't make them any less valid. Like that stubborn old shadow, the same reasons for the retreat—for becoming stalled—will still be there the next morning. This makes retreat a poor choice, like hibernation, because all we are losing is time.

Don't Come Near Me!

Grace, one of my former students, has chosen to stall. She came to see me to share how her closest friend undermined her by spreading nasty gossip at work. Grace said, "I never saw it coming. I shared an extremely sensitive family situation with her, and she told the entire office staff. Once I turned my back and left the room I could hear her giggle and laugh with the rest of them. It was so mean-spirited and hurtful. Betty Ann, my supposedly best friend, doing this to me. As far as I'm concerned, she's history. The verse from the O'Jays' song keeps playing over and over in my head: 'They smile in your face, all the time they wanna take your place, the backstabbers!' The next week Betty Ann came by my apartment to say she was sorry, and I slammed the door in her face. And I said, 'I don't want to ever talk to you again.'"

That day in my office Grace shared her feelings of surprise and disappointment, but mainly what came through in her tone, her body language, and her vehemence was betrayal and anger. I asked her how she is going to deal with her feelings and her relationship with Betty Ann. And she told me directly: "Betty Ann was the only real friend I ever had. I don't make friends that easily and now she has double-crossed me, big time. She hurt me! Badly! When I see her at work, I'll brush her off and ignore her. I will close the door and lock it."

Obviously, and quite understandably, Grace has been injured by betrayal and her hurt is overwhelming. Betrayal has caused a virtual emotional hurricane of hurt feelings in her life and there is no relief agency on the way to her with speedy recovery. It has rocked her world and it hit her like a ton of bricks putting her into "shut out" mode.

Once Grace and Betty Ann were the closest of friends; now they won't even stand in the same room with each other. Grace has decided to build walls, pull away, retreat, isolate, and distance herself from her best friend, instead of dancing to forgiveness. The only way to separate Grace from her angry feelings will be to literally pry her away from them.

We all know the purpose of building walls: to hide, separate, keep out, protect from further injury, feel safe and secure, and mark our boundaries. I think of the wall of my house, the walls of my bedroom, work room, office, and the sides of my car. The fence around my property is another kind of wall. The program on my computer that gets rid of bad e-mail is a kind of wall between myself and those who would unscrupulously send me a virus. Even my computer comes with a virtual wall between me and the outside world; the term "firewall" is a technical term for a program that keeps other people outside my house from using my computer.

Grace is putting up walls that may be difficult to scale, slowing forgiveness to a stall, and she's declaring the cold war—the silent treatment—which closes the door to any immediate resolution to heal her hurt.

It's strange how a friend can one day become our worst nightmare. Someone we thought we could trust who later turns out to be an unexpected enemy. When friends let us down and aren't there for us when we need them the most, it is a very personal betrayal. Sometimes the reason why they betray us is simply unknown; it may even forever remain a mystery. When we're at the receiving end of that kind of betrayal, we feel hurt, confused, and angry.

Friendship Breakdown

Friendship breakdown is something most of us have experienced but few of us really talk about. The hurt of a broken friendship can haunt us for years. Unfortunately, there is no crystal ball to predict that a particular friend will indeed turn out to be a reliable, positive influence in our lives or, by contrast, that a negative association will cause us emotional distress or worse.

When she was betrayed, Grace chose to cut herself off from Betty Ann and end their relationship. The talks with Betty Ann were over, phone calls were not returned, letters remained unanswered, and there was no contact whatsoever. Grace built a fortress around herself with no communication with Betty Ann; her own personal "firewall" is complete and far too effective.

The walls are there for a reason; they shut out the hurt, but they keep anger in. But at what point does the wall become a prison? If she continues building her wall high enough and long enough, the withdrawal and isolation will eventually end up hurting Grace more than Betty Ann. The pain will eat her up because she's not repairing it or releasing it.

Grace desperately needs to dance to forgiveness and learn to stop dwelling on the past. She must be determined to move on and move past the pain. In short, and I recognize this as a tall order for the still very upset Grace, she has to let go of the anger and the betrayal.

Obviously, one does not start dancing to forgiveness all of a sudden or, for that matter, all on one's own. Grace needs reassurance that her emotional health is important. Only then can she learn a better dance move: *knock down those walls!* She's learned to put them up; she can learn to knock them down. And if keeping her guard up to avoid being hurt next time is still important to Grace, she can even learn to put windows or doors in her walls. (Remember, offering forgiveness does not mean being a doormat!)

When we see walls in our relationships, we should immediately rent a jackhammer to get rid of them. When we do, we often forget why the walls went up in the first place.

Our walls do, however, have a purpose. Grace *needed* her walls because she was violated by Betty Ann's betrayal and didn't feel safe. Safety, not isolation, is Grace's biggest concern; that is where the source and the solution to her anxiety must be addressed. When Grace feels she is no longer in danger of being hurt, her walls will come down and she'll dance on.

I continually challenged and encouraged Grace to come out from behind those walls and consider the dance to forgiveness. I knew this was easier said than done for her, but I also knew it wasn't impossible. Seeing Grace months later, I asked her how she was doing. She said, "I broke through the walls. Something inside me told me there's hope for my relationship with Betty Ann. I want to mend this relationship. I don't want to be caught up in a seemingly never-ending roller coaster of anger and hurt."

This took time to accomplish, because Grace had nursed her anger and hurt for so long. But, she did knock down the walls, brick by brick. I often reflect on her vehemence when she first recounted her betrayal by Betty Ann. Time, discovery, and self-awareness have helped her put the situation in a better perspective. Witnessing the anger in her eyes and the scorn in her tone that day, I truly feel that if Grace can forgive, anyone can!

I Will Never Speak to You Again!

Brenda has a university colleague named Martha. During a faculty meeting in the spring, when Brenda and Martha came down on opposite sides of an issue, Martha took it as a personal attack. Shutdown soon began in earnest.

She later told me, "Martha jumped on everything I would say, typically taking stuff out of context or misunderstanding it and then ranting. Stranger to me, though, was the silent treatment; absolutely no acknowledgment of my presence. For some time I continued to say hello, in part to show human kindness. But I've given up on that lately. Another colleague told me that Martha also had a blowup with him, and they didn't speak for a year."

The silent treatment should not be confused with a "cooling off" period after we've been injured. In that case we're cooling off to catch a breath, to make sense of the injury, and to decide how we're going to respond; but the implication is clear, we'll respond at some point, and likely sooner rather than later.

The silent treatment is another animal altogether. In fact, there's a big difference between taking time to cool down and ignoring the existence of the other person. The silent treatment means we cease acknowledging someone or something that hurt us. Not for a short time, not until the "staring contest" is over and one of us blinks, not until one of us cracks a joke and says, "I can't believe we waited this long to make up!" The silent treatment is intended to be permanent toward the one who did the injuring. Nothing positive comes from this type of behavior.

There's a popular joke on the silent treatment. A husband and his wife were having some problems at home and were giving each other the cold shoulder. The next week, the husband realized that he would need his wife to wake him at 5 AM for an early morning business flight to Chicago. Not wanting to be the first to break the silence and lose, he wrote on a piece of paper, "Please wake me at 5 AM."

The next morning the husband woke up, only to discover it was 9 AM and that he had missed his flight. Furious, he was about to go and see why his wife hadn't woken him when he noticed a piece of paper by the bed.

The paper said, "It's 5 AM! Wake up!"

Obviously, the wife wasn't going to let a little thing like her husband's business trip interfere with her version of the silent treatment!

I was visiting my friend Bill and his family in the hospice unit of a local hospital. As I sat talking, a gentleman walked into the room. Bill stared up at the man walking toward him and began to cry. The visitor, who by then was also crying, leaned over the bed to embrace Bill.

After a few moments, the man, whose name turned out to be Ken, said to me, "Bill is my brother. We haven't spoken in over twenty-five years."

Caught by surprise, I said, "You're kidding me!"

"We had an argument over a piece of property," replied Ken. "We've been estranged from each other ever since."

"We shouldn't have let things go like this for so long," Bill said.

"No," Ken agreed. "It shouldn't take something like this—" at which point he gestured toward Bill's hospital bed, "to get us to come to our senses."

"You're right," Bill said. "Ken, you haven't met my children." Then Bill introduced his grown children to their uncle.

Why do we end up giving people the silent treatment? Partially, I think, it's for self-protection; because when we feel hurt, we just want the person to go away. We want to cut them out of our lives. We don't want to deal with them so we ignore them. We're so angry, we don't want to share our hurt, and so instead of trying to talk to about, we say nothing at all.

The problem with this strategy, of course, is that while we know our behavior is unhealthy, we're right about why we're so angry (and passionately so!). While not always accurate, we have ourselves convinced that the other person may apologize just for appearance's sake but never actually concede that they were wrong. The more intense our conviction, the longer we'll behave this way. Intelligence doesn't play into this; at this point, it's all about the emotions of pain, hurt, and revenge.

When shutdown dominates our lives, we engage in it totally, absolutely, and completely. But how counterproductive! The person who needs to see our hurt, pain, and disappointment the most is the one we're shutting out. We don't want him or her to know how hurt we are. If we need crying time, we do it at home, or in the bathroom, or in bed where *no one can see*. We don't answer his or her e-mails. And if we see that person, we avoid eye contact and offer the cold shoulder. We endure the silence. We loathe breaking it off—even when we're miserable.

Andrew and Donna have been having problems in their marriage of seventeen years. She finally left him. "It was a culmination of things," he admitted. "But I'm desperately trying to save our marriage."

Donna left their home in Wilkes-Barre, Pennsylvania, and went to her parents' home in Scottsdale, Arizona. She changed her cell phone number so he couldn't reach her. Her parents have blocked him from entering their gated community. So he sent her five dozen roses. He said: "All I want to do is talk, to ask for forgiveness, and to plead for the chance for us to work on our relationship." So far Andrew has had no response from Donna.

The unanswered question remains. Will Donna ever relent? How long can she go on with the silent treatment and, for his part, how long will Andrew seek forgiveness before he moves on? And, if Donna waits long enough to break her silence, will it be too late?

As we have seen, the silent treatment can be hurtful, frustrating, and confusing *to both parties*. It's a way of getting even and of punishing people who have injured us by making them feel our hurt. It shows our displeasure for what they have done to us by permanently freezing them out of our lives and treating them as if they don't exist or, for that matter, never did.

Thaw Out or Freeze Out?

Some people choose to keep their injured relationship on ice, not for therapeutic purposes to soothe the ache, but to continue to shut out and shut down by ceasing to talk to the person who harmed them and pretending they no longer matter.

When we continue to build higher walls and carry on the silent treatment, we hit our relationship with blasts of arctic air which thickens, strengthens, and deepens the already thick ice of hopelessness. Now we're faced with massive chunks of Antarctica ice and a choice: to *thaw out* or *freeze out*.

Choosing to thaw out the injured relationship breaks the ice and allows for our movement to forgiveness. Until we decide to turn up the heat, we stay stuck and keep the wound open. We can delay the thaw for months or even years before we dance to forgiveness. We keep tripping over our pride and feel that any sign of melting the ice and letting the person off the hook is a sure sign of weakness. So, distance is maintained, avoidance is practiced, and communication is silent.

Until we make an attempt to thaw, the infected wound intensifies. The slightest mention of the person who caused the injury throws salt on it, worsening it, and raises the anger level, making us vulnerable to damaging our minds and bodies, as well as our emotions.

Patrick and William work at a large internet company together. Patrick frequently gossips and damages the reputation of William and his family. William, despite being a Christian, seeks to get even. Deciding against public confrontation, he attacks Patrick secretly. William gives him the cold shoulder and places gossip in the right ears. Patrick realizes what he did was wrong and comes remorsefully to William to apologize and move on with his life.

Instead, William tells Patrick, "This is war and you drew first blood. That's that. We're finished." William continues to seethe about Patrick's actions. He thinks about it on his drive home, while he's feeding his baby son, and before he goes to sleep. When he sees Patrick at work, it gets even worse; he swells with anger.

The situation preoccupies William 24/7/365. His anger becomes an obsession. He stops attending church. His wife and children wonder why he is often moody, jumpy, and angry at home. His blood pressure rises; he develops an ulcer and sleeps less.

Unbeknownst to Patrick, he's haunting William day and night. Patrick has apologized and forgotten about the event, yet William has allowed Patrick to take over his life and be a permanent (and unwelcome) guest in his head.

This is the scenario when we choose to put a relationship on ice. While Patrick said some hurtful words (and admitted to saying them), William has a choice: thaw out or freeze out—give himself a life sentence which will destroy his health and damage his relationship with his wife, children, friends, and coworkers, or open the door and let the sun melt the ice.

In 1980 Jimmy Carter was running for president of the United States against Ronald Reagan. According to David Wallis in the *New York Times Magazine*, prior to a televised debate between the candidates, columnist George Will discovered a copy of Carter's debate notes and passed them along to the Reagan camp.

Many political analysts said that Reagan won the debate, and he went on to win the election. Carter learned what Will had done and despite his seemingly gentle and wise nature, did not forget it or forgive him.

In a 1997 interview with Wallis, Carter said,

> I was teaching forgiveness one day in Sunday school, and I tried to go through my memory about people for whom I had a resentment. George Will was one of those people, so I wrote him a note. I asked myself, "What do we have in common?" and I had known that he had written a book about baseball, which I had refused to read. I went to a bookstore and found a secondhand copy. I paid a dollar for it. So I wrote him a note and told him the facts and that I had a feeling of resentment toward him, that I had found his book delightful, and I hoped that we would be permanently reconciled. [Will] wrote me back a nice, humorous note. He said his only regret was that I didn't pay full price for his book.

Having sat many hours with many injured people, they told me they also had to choose to thaw out because keeping the relationship on ice was causing them frost bite and they realized they couldn't continue the way they were going—they had to dance to forgiveness or freeze to death!

Several people told me that once they made that decision, their lives almost instantly got better. The anger went away, the stress went away. Margaret, whose daughter was brutally raped, actually confessed, "As hard as it was to let the rapist off my hook, I had to move toward forgiveness or it would have killed me. Forgiveness allowed me to get on with living."

Keeping the Walls Up

When our dance moves includes the dance of "freeze out," we

place the injured relationship in an inflexible situation and live with the motto: "End it, but never mend it." We keep the walls up, the memory fresh, telling ourselves, "I'll never forget...."

The grudge is frozen: "I'm going to stay angry."

The gossip is flying: "Well, let me tell you about..."

At this point, we would rather die than forgive. There are no second chances. Just the idea of letting go and moving on is inconceivable and impossible for us. We allow all the old stuff to get in the way of new stuff that could bring healing and comfort. Even when we know we're the one suffering the most, the "comfort" of nursing our old grudges is preferable to the opportunity of hope and joy that new experiences bring.

Joan told me told she divorced Ray eight years ago. She does everything she can to make it difficult for him to see the children. When she speaks of Ray, she's still angry, bitter, and resentful. Ray has moved on with his life and is settled in a new relationship. Joan hasn't gotten past the hurt.

In one of our sessions, I said, "Joan, look who you have become. People want to avoid you. Your family is tired of hearing about Ray. He's living his life and you are still stuck in what happened years ago."

Ray has said a number of times, "I'm sorry. What I did was wrong."

She only says, "I will never, ever, forgive him."

I ask you, who is suffering more?

When I was first ordained a priest, I believed that over fifty percent of all problems were at least in part due to the refusal to forgive. After ten years in ministry, I revised my estimate and maintained that seventy-five to eighty percent of all health, marital, family, and financial problems came from the refusal to forgive. Now, after more than twenty-five years in ministry, I've concluded that over ninety percent of all problems are rooted in unforgiveness, which is a direct result of our choosing to shut out, shut down, and freeze out, leaving people out in the bitter cold and giving ourselves emotional frostbite in return!

We've all been hurt at some level, but what do we do when those hurts feel insurmountable or unforgivable? First, we can realize that they aren't insurmountable or unforgivable; we have choices. We can choose to keep dancing the retreat step over and over or decide to move on.

Healing and forgiveness don't take place by shutting out, shutting down, or freezing out. These moves only push the pain away and block us from fully experiencing forgiveness and healing, which can only happen when we decide to thaw out. Only then can we move on to restore and repair our injured relationship, bringing us beyond a place of hurt, to a place of joy and fulfillment—where we can use our hurts to heal others. That's why we need to get on our feet, find our way back to the dance floor, and dance to forgiveness.

Jesus tells us that we are to forgive not just once, twice, or even seven times but *seventy times seven*. That's 490 times! Most of us find it hard to forgive just the one affront. How can we ever manage the other 489?

Obviously Jesus is serious about forgiveness. In his parable of the unforgiving debtor, he described three scenes illustrating the three applications of the story. Scene one portrays the largest debt ever incurred (150,000 years' wages) being forgiven, or let go, from the king to his servant. Scene two paints a similar scenario; however, the debt incurred between the forgiven servant and his fellow servant is comparatively quite small (a hundred days' wages).

The servant who had been forgiven the largest debt ever incurred will not let go of the small debt with his fellow servant. He wants to hold on. Scene three casts a dark reality. Word of the forgiven servant's behavior reaches the king, who responds by throwing the unforgiving servant into prison. Jesus concluded the parable with quite possibly the most sobering words in Scripture, "This is how my heavenly Father will treat each of you unless you forgive each other from your heart" (Matthew 18:35).

We're all eager to receive forgiveness but we're sometimes unwilling to give it. That's the whole point of Jesus' parable. So, if you're having trouble forgiving someone, I suggest you read (or reread) this parable carefully.

Something to Consider (Ponder)

As you can tell, I love movies. You remember the movie *Rain Man* (1988) with Dustin Hoffman and Tom Cruise; they play brothers. Tom Cruise is the younger brother and Dustin Hoffman is an older, autistic brother. Cruise takes his brother on a cross-country road trip in the hope of rebuilding a relationship that may or may not have existed to begin with.

Raymond, Dustin Hoffman's character, makes note of everything that happens along the way. One time Tom Cruise's character, Charlie Babbitt, gets angry with him and grabs Raymond by the scruff of the neck. Raymond recorded it: "Charlie Babbitt squeezed and pulled and hurt my neck."

He actually keeps a journal of these offenses; a running log of who and what offended him. Some of us actually keep a journal, but how many people keep a journal of *offenses*? I'm sure hardly any of us does, but what we do is keep those offenses right in our hearts, just in case we have to pull them out one day and say: "Here, see; this is why I built these walls. This is why I shut you out. This is why I gave you the silent treatment for two years!! Don't you remember? I do; I have it all written down here in my heart." You might ask yourself at this point:

- Am I angry with anyone today?
- What does it take to bring down the walls once I decide to dance toward forgiveness?

- How did it feel to finally thaw the ice and warm up my injured relationship?

- Did I get angry with anyone this past week?

- After I have hurt someone and have tried to talk about the relationship, but had the door slammed in my face, how did I feel? What did I do?

- Is there someone in my life who has hurt me and I have not forgiven?

- Even if I have been wronged, do I think that the silent treatment would correct things?

Something to Do (Practice)

Has someone lied about you? Stolen your promotion? Taken credit for the work you did? Is she guilty of flirting with your husband? Betraying a confidence? Spreading a rumor about your child? Forgiveness is difficult even to consider under such circumstances; I know, and I've heard it all by now. Yet the burden of scorn, anger, or hatred is so heavy that it literally warps the soul. Endure such pain for long enough and your soul will never quite fit right again. Better to pray for strength to forgive than the chance to get even.

Try a simple experiment on yourself. Make a fist and hold it tight. One minute of this is sufficient to bring discomfort. Consider what would happen if the fist were maintained in that state of tension during a period of weeks, months, or even years. Obviously it would soon become a sick member of the body, atrophying to the point of disuse—or worse, needing medical attention and possible amputation.

You may hurt a person by not forgiving him or her and thus feel the satisfying sense of getting even, but almost without exception, the hurt you do to yourself may be (is quite possibly) even greater. After a while you may not even feel the resentment in your soul, but its self-inflicted paralysis will have its effect upon your whole life, and eventually it will be your soul and not the offender's that atrophies.

Here's a way to picture what a frozen heart does. Take an empty glass. (Use a large tumbler or several glasses, or even a fish bowl, depending on your injured list!) Next, on slips of paper write the names of those who have injured you, anyone you have shut out by refusing to forgive. Now, fill the glass with water and put it in the freezer. As long as the water is frozen, you can't retrieve the paper. As long as your heart is frozen, you can't offer forgiveness. And so you are left with a decision. Do you take the glass out of the freezer and thaw it out—or do you leave it there?

> *"When we can't forgive, we will break the bridge over which we must pass."*
>
> GEORGE HERBERT

Something to Say (Prayer)

Compassionate God, I need wisdom when I am injured in a relationship. Help me not to embrace my hurts so completely and tightly that I shut out others by putting up walls and shut down others by giving them the cold shoulder.

When I am hurt, give me the strength to be compassionate and forgiving, understanding and caring, rather than cutting others off and breaking all ties.

You know my pain and my human desire to get even and make the offender feel my pain. Help me not to do this. Help me to be wise. Help me to be open and reasonable and willing to talk things through.

I want to have more peaceful relationships, less conflict, less strife, less arguing, and more love, joy, and peace. Please give me the gift of wisdom. In Jesus' name, I pray. Amen.

❧ STEP 3 ❧

Revenge
Wanting Payback

"You have heard it said: An eye for an eye and tooth for a tooth." ❧ MATTHEW 5:38

The American humorist Josh Billings once said, "There is no revenge as complete as forgiveness." But if your heart is full of vengeance, anger, betrayal, and pain, such a quote—no matter how wise and accurate it may seem upon reflection—likely leaves you scoffing at the naïveté of its author.

Revenge is like that; it blinds us to the better sense of others, of literature, of great thinkers, of our pastors and parish priests, our families and friends, even ourselves, and even the teaching of Jesus in the gospels. It has been said that revenge is also the great equalizer; it makes fools of us all, and gives power to those against whom we seek it.

Something to Learn (Path)

As we have seen, life is full of hurtful relationships; they are everywhere and, in our modern society, impossible to avoid. People get crushed, betrayed, abused, manipulated, ignored, bruised, broken, and wounded in ways they never see coming. When we're shocked by such abuse, we often react in ways that aren't quite our normal way of acting.

Rosemary's life completed changed when she got hit by a car, spent the night in a trauma unit, and several months in recovery at home. She's grateful for the fact that she has fully recovered from her accident, but instead of celebrating that fact, she has focused on the people who disappointed her throughout her ordeal.

She said to me, "My 'perfect' boyfriend that lived two hours away didn't care enough to come visit, even though he could have, and the same with my 'best' friend that lived in the same town. I basically just had my sister to take care of me, because all our family lives in California. The whole incident made me see that people are selfish, immature, inconsiderate, and completely ignorant. I have since broken up with my boyfriend and I never want to see his face again. And I also cut off all contact with my best friend."

"Everyone agrees that they are both creeps," she concluded. "I hope when they're in my shoes, the same thing happens to them, and when it does, I'll throw a party for myself and enjoy singing 'What comes around, goes around.'"

Before we're too harsh with this angry woman bent on revenge, we need to ask ourselves a few questions: How prone are we to harbor a grudge? How inclined to get even when injured? How quick to take offense?

As human beings, when we experience enormous hurt in our lives or prolonged hurt or repeated hurt, we develop a pocket of anger and bitterness inside, and if this pocket is not lanced and drained, it backs up and poisons us.

Don't believe me? Just look at how we label revenge: "Nursing a grudge." "Harboring a hurt." "Storing up grievances." "Paying back." "Blowing your stack." "Keeping score." All of these phrases point to a build-up, an overflow, a harmful release. Nevertheless, we take great pleasure in seeking revenge when we've been injured by someone. "Nothing is quite as sweet as getting even," one saying goes. Rosemary asked me, "What's wrong with some good, old-fashioned revenge? These people hurt me badly. I'm going to enjoy hearing that my ex-boyfriend and best friend have suffered a disaster or defeat alone."

Despite the sense they obviously made to her, Rosemary's vengeful statements left me shaking in disbelief. I shared with her that she's already shut out, shut down, and frozen out her boyfriend and best friend; so now she's allowing them to hurt her twice: once in the initial injury and then by the long-term pain it causes.

The "Power" of Payback

There's something inside us that enjoys the idea of getting even. I suspect that whenever others hurt us the temptation is there to immediately start thinking about what we can do to get back at them so *they* can see what it feels like. We love to inflict the hurt we feel just to pay the offender back…with interest.

Tammy and Doug had been married for twenty-five years. It was one of those marriages that are not so good and not so bad. But over time, the love between the two of them gradually dissolved. Eventually, Doug had an affair and that pretty much ended the marriage. They divorced, leaving her with the four children. She ended up much poorer than she thought she was going to be. There just wasn't enough money to pay all the bills and this caused her much inner turmoil.

Doug soon remarried. "Too soon," or so it felt to Tammy. But it was the wedding day of their youngest daughter that finally got to her. That "other woman" was escorted down the aisle, and seated right behind her. The inner rage started. And when her husband came down the aisle, smiling ear to ear with their daughter, well, that was just too much. Nobody knew what she was feeling, of course; she covered it up with appropriate smiles, greeting others as if they were all just one big, happy family. But that defining moment in the church on the wedding day of her daughter was one of the most difficult times of her whole life.

She later confessed, "There isn't a day I don't think of ways to get back at him for the spectacle he pulled at our daughter's wedding. If it takes me the rest of my life, *he's gonna pay.*"

How often those words have been uttered in my office. "He's gonna pay." "She's gonna pay." I call it the not-so-subtle re-routing of our positive life force for negative means. It's like this person was going along, living his or her life, and suddenly that defining moment happened, calling for revenge.

Suddenly, all the power they used to run their lives before—to go shopping, work hard, earn a living, be happy, solid, productive citizens—got "re-routed" to this new place of anger, hate, betrayal, and revenge. Now all their energy goes toward "payback."

In the movies, of course, payback is an enjoyable plot device. Who doesn't like seeing the "good guy" get even with the bad guys for killing his wife and kids? Or to see hapless victims get away from a masked serial killer and exact some kind of revenge of their own, all before the final credits!

When the good guy gets revenge, we leave the theater happy and content; that's how life is supposed to be. When the bad guy wins, or the masked killer can't be stopped no matter how much we were rooting for the victims, the movie makers call it a "twist," but for the audience it was a bad ending.

Life, of course, isn't like the movies. We can't take a machine gun and sneak up on the bad guys and spray the room with bullets. There are rules and laws to obey and in fact in real life it's not even possible to get revenge. Yet we stay stuck in the thought and the hope of revenge.

At one time or another we've all wanted revenge; admit it. Just ask yourself these three questions and see if you can say "no" with a clear conscience:

- Do you ever bring up old issues that someone has already asked your forgiveness for?

- Is there anyone you consistently treat coolly who has injured you?

- Did you ever think of ways to hurt those who have hurt you?

Revenge is everywhere. No person is immune from the temptation. As a result, we build up poisonous feelings and hold on to unresolved issues that can never be brought to closure. When old wounds aren't fully healed, they become infected and healing begins to fade. Our "revenge dance" is a vicious movement to hurt the one who hurt us. But it ends up hurting us instead.

A Dangerous Choice

As anger festers within, resentment grows; then the desire for revenge becomes attractive. Revenge is a very powerful emotion that leads us to do extreme things. Wars have been started, lovers have been killed, affairs have been had, and relationships have been destroyed—all in the name of revenge.

If you doubt the truth of the above statement, simply look at your local newspaper. Read it closely, and you will find within its pages—more often than not closer to the front page—exquisitely planned and horribly painful tales of revenge, betrayal, hurt, and suffering; nearly every day.

The husband who drives his car through his ex-wife's house, killing everyone inside. The wife who runs over her ex, and keeps running him over, despite a dozen witnesses and just as many parking lot security cameras. The child who kills his parents; the mother who sacrifices her child to get even with her husband.

And yet these are no movie villains or masked killers, just normal, everyday people, housewives, entrepreneurs, businessmen and women who harbored poisonous revenge for so long, or felt so hurt so strongly, that the overflow of powerful emotions spilled over into violent plots of revenge.

Clearly, some people plot out intricate, detailed strategies for righting injuries and settling scores. They don't simply retaliate in a subtle way. They fight back, no matter who gets hurt. It's not enough to get revenge or right a wrong; they want that ultimate payback of making that other person feel the pain they felt, and then some.

A disgruntled employee sabotages the company because he feels slighted or mistreated. Someone gets angry at a coworker and undermines his or her effectiveness by circulating a vicious rumor. A former boyfriend now dates a woman you always despised. All of it boils down to revenge.

People who have been friends for years stop speaking to one another. Family members are alienated. There's bad blood between departments in your company, families in the neighborhood, or people who are members of your parish church and it lingers for months, years, or decades. The greater our desires to seek revenge on those who have injured us, the greater the distance grows and the quicker communication dies and relationships end up in cold storage.

Why do we want to dance to the tune of revenge? Do we want someone to be fired? Someone's heart to break? Someone to embarrass? Someone to make jealous? Someone to feel the pain we've felt? Why do we want these things?

"Addicted" to Revenge

Revenge perpetuates the hurt; it's the mother of all snowball effects. It takes the injury and keeps it going. It prolongs the pain, drags it out, magnifies it, and makes it continually bigger in our (damaged) hearts and minds. We practice revenge because we think by getting even we can hurt those who injured us.

The funny thing about revenge is that at first it feels powerful and satisfying. These feelings however, soon turn to regret, sadness, shame, and guilt. Unfortunately, by this time the damage has been done. The revenge is then bittersweet.

It's not unlike drug addiction. That first toke, snort, or whiff makes one feel powerful, bold, pain-free, and exuberant. Addicts love the feeling so much they want it more often. Eventually, they have to keep taking more to get the original high. Then they have to keep taking more just so they don't feel worse. In either case, revenge or drug addiction, the once-positive euphoria or high is long gone and all that's left is a shell of what once was. It's important to remember that although we may have been injured or embarrassed (or *fill in your own blank here*), this does not give us the right to do the same to others. Revenge is not a healthy action, no matter how justified we feel.

Moving On Is Key

Maybe you heard about the Desert Storm soldier who while he was overseas received a "Dear John" letter from his girlfriend back home. To add insult to injury, she wrote, "Will you please return my favorite photograph of myself; I need it for my engagement picture in the local newspaper."

The poor guy was devastated, but all the soldiers came to his rescue. They went throughout the entire camp and collected pictures of all the guys' girlfriends. They filled up an entire shoe box and sent it back to the girl, along with a note from the guy saying, "Please find your picture, and return the rest; for the life of me, I can't remember which one is you!"

Humorous, fitting, and at the same time apparently harmless! I call it relatively harmless because, as far as I understand, that's where it ended; she hurt him, he hurt her back, his friends helped him to heal and she probably opened the box, realized it was her "just desert," married her new guy, and moved on with her life. Moving on is key: If they both moved on, the dual acts of tit and tat were harmless and, in many ways, cathartic. A healthy blowout and then back to normal life.

Unfortunately, in far too many cases, we can become obsessed with "winning at any cost." Our anger increases and reaches an explosive level because the person who injured us isn't chasing after us or seeking us out to repair the relationship. After the initial hurt was dealt, they may have even communicated a desire to sit down and talk this out and even made multiple attempts to forgive, but we've responded with the "retreat" dance moves: shut out, shut down, and freeze out. We've ignored their offers of apology or attempts to reconcile, and it should have stopped there. Instead WE perpetuated the hurt and focus on revenge. "Notice me!" we seem to be shouting. "I'm still here! I'm still hurting! You should be hurting too!"

Despite our better judgment, something in us wants them to come crawling back on their hands and knees begging for forgiveness, but they aren't doing that, which makes us even more angry.

Revenge is a poor substitute for wisdom; it is short-sighted, counterproductive, and ineffective. Revenge upon someone who hurts us only deals with a single situation. Forgiveness clears our vision and helps us see how we were drawn into an injured relationship to begin with. It helps us recognize other situations that could lead to hurt feelings. Dancing toward forgiveness frees our own souls. It lets us out of prison. It lets us continue to grow into tender-hearted and affectionate people. And it keeps us from holding people hostage, from shaking our fists, striking back in vengeful fury, or putting others on probation until they have felt our pain.

Forgiveness frees our minds and souls and helps us to remember that those who hurt us can never win as long as we don't allow them to remain the focus of our living. Once we forgive, we can focus once again on becoming wise, loving, and kind people.

Please understand, forgiveness is not another word for stupidity; it doesn't make you a doormat. If someone has injured you, forgiving them doesn't mean you excuse, condone, or for that matter forget what they have done. What forgiveness *does* mean is that you no longer wait for others to pay for what they have done to you. You move on with your life, becoming who you were meant to be.

And there's another beautiful benefit of forgiveness. People seem almost magically drawn to learn from those who have triumphed over hurt and become more loving as a result.

Forgiving someone who hurt us really is the sweetest form of "revenge." Not because we've given up or even given in, but because we've truly given ourselves permission to reclaim our lives, learn from the experience, and move on. Once we have released our desire for revenge, the one who injured us no longer has power over us.

A Worthless Cause

There's a line near the end of *Camelot* that stuck in my mind the first time I heard it. As King Arthur surveys the ruin and carnage of war, he looks forlornly over the landscape and laments that revenge is "the most worthless of causes."

Unfortunately, the lesson seems destined to be learned only by those who have come to the sad truth themselves. As a result, countless wars have been fought to avenge tarnished honor. Friendships have been destroyed, marriages broken apart, and children set against their parents for this most worthless of causes.

Simply because it leads to such terrible outcomes, most of the great ethical teachers through the centuries have rebuked the urge to retaliate. Jesus, the greatest teacher, not only taught his followers to let offenses pass—to turn the other cheek—but to forgive our enemies. He said to return good for evil.

Charlotte Brontë wrote, "Life appears to me too short to be spent in nursing animosity or registering wrong."

Rather than seeking revenge, we could choose to get in touch with our hurts and then dance the healthy steps of repair and release that lead to forgiveness. When we choose to dance these steps and to be self-responsible, an interesting phenomenon occurs: We let go of getting even. We are suddenly free to reroute the negative energy we've been dealing with for so long and put it to a more positive use in our lives.

Revenge is truly self-defeating. We can eliminate our need for payback by practicing self-reflection and living intentionally from a place of understanding, empathy, compassion, and forgiveness. This is not to say that we condone true and real injury, but rather take a deep and conscious look at the hold revenge has on us and learn how to release that hold.

In the end the old cliché is true: Don't cut off your nose to spite your face. Revenge is needless; it's a worthless reaction to an injury that ends up causing more damage to ourselves than to the one who hurt us in the first place.

Something to Consider (Ponder)

In the movie *Fried Green Tomatoes* (1991), a middle-aged woman in a big expensive car was waiting to pull into a long-awaited parking space. Suddenly, a young girl in a small sports car zoomed in ahead of her. The woman angrily asked why she had done that. The young woman's response was, "Face it lady, we're younger and faster!" and with that she entered the store.

When she came back out a few minutes later, she found the older woman using her big car as a battering ram, backing up, and repeatedly ramming her little car. The young woman very angrily asked the offender why she was wrecking her precious sports car. The older woman's response? "Face it, I'm older, and I have more insurance!"

Although many aspects of revenge resemble or echo the concept of making things equal, revenge usually has a more injurious goal.

If you feel that you are harboring revengeful feelings, consider these questions:

> *"An eye for an eye makes the whole world blind."*
>
> MAHATMA GANDHI

- Where and how did I learn to "get back" at others for injuries in my life?

- What was my experience of revenge and "getting even" like when I was growing up?

- Am I the type of person who doesn't just get mad...I get even? Why?

- Do I keep mental notes of all the people who have hurt me in life?

- Do I believe that two wrongs make a right?

- Have I gotten revenge on someone in the last six months? Have I thought about it?

Although you may not like your own answers, this healthy, conscious, and deeper process of inquiry can support you to move from a place of revenge to a place of well-being where you can take control of your life by taking back your power and giving up being a "victim."

Something to Do (Practice)

Use "Snap It to Stop It Therapy" (otherwise known as "rubber-band therapy") to stop revenge. Wear a rubber band around your wrist for each person you're hoping to pay back. Every time the thought of revenge pops in your head, snap the rubber band (ouch!) to catch yourself. This is a visual clue as well. If you have more than one or two rubber bands on your wrist, you may be so addicted to revenge that it's taking over your life.

Something to Say (Prayer)

Compassionate God, teach me to turn toward your forgiving heart each time someone hurts me, whether deliberate or not. Strengthen me to turn to you when things aren't going my way or when I'm frustrated and feeling like I've been "kicked around" long enough.

Give me patience and restraint when I'm ready to fight back, to get my revenge. Let me turn to you, O God, and move away from the circle of revenge and start dancing to forgiveness. I have spent too much time thinking about how to strike back and too little time trying to open new doors of forgiveness and repair. Strengthen my weakness. In Jesus' name, I pray. Amen.

❧ STEP 4 ❧

Rehearse
Telling Everybody

"If your brother sins, go and show him his fault in private; if he listens to you, you have won your brother."   ❧ MATTHEW 18:15

Dance step four, *Rehearse*, now completes the repertoire of steps that further stall our dance to forgiveness. Dance these steps long enough, hard enough, and dance them alone, and you may find yourself in a permanent state of despair.

What, exactly, does it mean to "rehearse"? When we rehearse the hurt we are feeling, we replay the scene over and over in our minds and relay it to anyone who will listen to us. We've all been on the receiving end of someone else's revenge rehearsal, and it's not enjoyable.

Something that happened years ago can still sting as deeply as if it happened yesterday, because we are constantly *rehearsing* the details. As a result, we can never get past it.

For instance, consider a woman whose husband left her. She remembers exactly what type of shirt he had on the day he left.

She remembers the cutting words he said. She remembers how he told her he didn't love her anymore. She has focused on that setting, that scene, so many times, repetitiously, until the details are etched in living color.

When we keep telling people "I can never forgive this person," "I can never get over this hurt," "I was hurt so badly," we become a walking wound staggering under the weight of anger and revenge. It can really take a toll on us physically, emotionally, and spiritually and, if we dance this step long enough, it may just end up putting us in an early grave.

Something to Learn (Path)

Claudia and Janet were best friends and they promised one another that when they got married, each would be the other's maid of honor. When the time came, however, Janet chose someone else. Claudia was hurt and confused.

She told me, "Janet didn't even tell me, and when my invitation arrived, I threw it to the floor. That good-for-nothing couldn't *make* me go to her wedding! A tsunami of hurt and anger suddenly overwhelmed me. I stamped around all that week in a rage and plotted all sorts of nasty things, from writing a rude letter to not buying a gift, anything to get back at her. I made myself thoroughly miserable with fits of anger and indignation. I called just about everybody on my contact list to tell them what Janet had done to me."

Although Claudia was still in the early stages of *rehearsal*, she was well on her way to being an expert in "telling everybody"! Why did Claudia respond this way? Why was her anger so sudden; why was her first response to tell the world how she had been wronged?

The questions are many; the answers are few. The fact is, telling everybody is a big part of the rehearsal itself. The more people we tell, the more real it becomes. Unfortunately, the more real it becomes and the longer we hold onto the tiniest of details, the more we put ourselves and our health at risk. Research has shown that there are definite biological links between hostility and anger and the increased risk of certain diseases like coronary heart disease. On the other hand, positive emotions like forgiveness and love seem to enhance physical health.

Yet, we still choose to dance this step.

Circle the Wagons

When we feel hurt, we pull away from the important people in our lives. We distance ourselves in an effort to protect ourselves from more pain and injury. We might keep ourselves busy and away from the person(s) who hurt us. We don't open ourselves up to sharing what is on our minds and in our hearts anymore— except that one incident. We withdraw our warmth and affection. We stop investing our time in giving and nurturing our relationships. We just keep dwelling on our injury, and every time we tell the story, the wound becomes deeper and dancing to forgiveness becomes a more remote possibility.

We stop waiting for people to respond and ignore the fact that the response is no longer positive. We ignore the fact that people are avoiding us, doing anything to get away quickly, mentioning that they may have heard this same story "a time or two" before.

How long can this last? I had some great aunts who, well into their eighties, would occasionally bring up some incident or other involving one of the sisters. They were still angry about whatever the injury was, still pushed out of shape by it, still holding a grudge, and still rehearsing something that happened more than fifty years earlier!

This is not unusual. In fact, there's quite a market for rehearsing hurts in my work as a chaplain. I have seen so many people over the years who spend an enormous amount of time going over in greater and greater detail, just how their parents hurt them. Sadly, this pain is so affecting and the rehearsal so intense that it's as if the adult never quite left childhood; their development stopped the day of the hurt and, in many ways, they are frozen in time, doomed to rehearse those events in perpetuity.

In the classic movie *On Golden Pond* (1991), Jane Fonda plays a character named Chelsea who is forever bitter toward her father, played by her real-life father, Henry Fonda. Toward the end of the movie her mother, played by Katharine Hepburn, tired of Chelsea's bitterness and eager to see her come to grips with it and move on, tells her, "You're a big girl now. Aren't you tired of it all? Bore, bore." And, just a little later, she says, "Life marches by, Chels. I suggest you get on with it."

The fact is, truly awful hurts *will* affect us negatively for the rest of our lives, unless we "get on with it." They will never cease to have happened, but they will fade in intensity the farther out in time we get from them and more eager we are to dance to forgiveness and repair them—unless we keep them alive by rehearsing them to anyone who will listen.

Dancing to forgiveness doesn't mean that we pretend nothing bad has ever happened to us. It doesn't discount the hurt that we've been through. It doesn't mean "getting over it" before we've even had time to process it. It does mean, however, that we have to stop rehearsing and stop dwelling on it.

Why after being injured in the first place, whether it was as a child or adult, do we have to continue to suffer by rehearsing our hurt? Some people say, "Because I don't want to give him or her the satisfaction of forgiveness." But, I believe the answer is choreographed in two movements *dwell* and *tell*, causing the relationship to swell and never get well.

Always on My Mind: Dwell

We've all heard the expression, time heals all wounds, but for people who choose to dance the retreat, revenge, and rehearse repertoire, time is stalled or stopped. Time does pass from minute to minute, hour to hour, but it is not being used wisely during such dance routines.

Although time may pass, people who have been injured choose to dwell on the hurt (keeping their emotions forever in neutral) and decide to say things and do things that deepen the wound, making it difficult to repair.

A gentleman told me that his wife had ongoing extramarital affairs, which eventually ended their marriage. These were the facts, as ugly as they might have been: extramarital affairs + betrayal = failed marriage. But...he keeps dwelling on the hurt. He replays the sequence of events over and over in his mind and retells the incident to anyone who will listen. He told me, "One day I will wake up and realize with hindsight, as is always the case, I wasted precious time."

Have you ever heard the expression, "He wears his heart on his sleeve"? That's what I think of when I hear people dwelling on the hurt and telling everyone within earshot. These people are such open wounds, the hurt is so raw and ever present—even if it happened years ago or in childhood. The minute anyone takes the slightest interest in them or gives them the tiniest opening, it all just comes gushing out in a tidal wave of hurt, bitterness, and remorse.

I see and hear it far too often these days. For most of us, if someone asks, "How are you?" our reply is vaguely general, such as "Just fine" or "Feeling great" or, at worst, "Got a cold; but getting over it!"

For these people, this innocent greeting opens the door to an avalanche. "Well, if you call being repeatedly cheated on by your wife and then being dumped, with the judge giving her the house anyway fine, I guess you could say I'm doing fine!"

I often think that dwelling on our hurt is similar to a stranglehold we have on a person whose actions we ultimately can't control. Whatever the hurt is, we've wrestled it to the ground and we're holding on for dear life. But it's our lives we are choking out, not those of the offender. And without help, intervention, or understanding, we'll continue strangling the life out of our own life until there's literally nothing left.

No one can say what the acceptable amount of time for hurt and bitterness should be. For one person, it's two weeks; for another, it could be two months. Do we put a time limit on how long a person who has been violated, robbed, mugged, or had a family member killed should feel bitter and upset? Hardly.

So perhaps we will never know the proper length of time to hold onto hurt. What we *do* know for sure is that by dwelling on it so that it takes up all the space in our hearts and minds, it becomes a barrier that closes out all peace of mind. As we have said, by dwelling on the hurt, we're actually giving the offender the power to hurt us again and again and again. Every day we rehearse the hurt, unleash the venom on some unsuspecting bystander, or belabor the point to family and friends, we are reliving it and allowing the offender to hurt us once more. What's worse, the offender is usually oblivious or apathetic.

Dwelling on injuries caused by disappointments, petty annoyances, lies, rumors, betrayals, insensitivity, and anger is like driving our car with both feet on the brake, our eyes on the rearview mirror, and our gas tank empty. We're wondering why we aren't moving forward, and yet all the while we're focused on the wrong direction! Even if you want to make progress, dwelling on our hurts keeps us in emotional limbo and stalls us or stops us from embracing profound forgiveness.

I love what playwright and actor Tyler Perry (who turned his life around when he stopped rehearsing a hurt that burned within him from childhood) has to say about forgiveness. It's short and powerful. If you still have intense anger in your heart for someone who hurt you recently or long ago, and you're still rehearsing, rehashing, reliving, or replaying it each and every chance you get, I encourage you to take Tyler's words seriously. I can't get over how powerful his statement is: "When you haven't forgiven those who've hurt you, you turn your back against your future. When you do forgive, you start walking forward."

We need to be aware always that it's our choice to keep dancing the same routine over and over, or break out a new one. Why not? If the steps you've been dancing for so long aren't working, change the CD, clear the floor, and try something new! We don't need to be afraid to try a new routine. We don't forget what was done to us, but we stop allowing the hurt to possess us.

Keep Spreading the News: Tell

When we keep telling everyone about an injury we have received, the repetition has a significant impact on our minds and bodies. In other words, *telling* about the hurt can be extremely taxing and the stress of it can actually shave years off our lives.

But, when revenge is our motivation, we choose to do it anyway. Inside us there is turmoil. The injury follows us 24/7. Peace evades us, and we secretly plot revenge as a payback. And so we continue to tell everyone we meet about what happened. Our goal is to make the offender look as offensive as possible so others turn against him or her. We feel better, he or she hurts. In our minds, everybody gets what they deserve.

Why do we carry our hurt stories from person to person? Why do we refuse to forgive an injury from the past, perhaps years ago or even when we were children? Maybe we're looking for sympathy. Maybe others will say that we're really good persons who don't deserve such injustice. Maybe they will pat us on the back and marvel at our holding up under such a hurtful situation.

But if we constantly rehearse our hurt to everybody we see, people will eventually get tired of hearing it. They may avoid us; see us coming and head in a different direction, thinking, "What's the matter with him? He should stop doing that to himself."

Warning: Do Not Open

I received an e-mail the other day that said those very words, "Warning: Do not open!" It told about a computer virus that could potentially destroy the entire hard drive on the computer. You have probably received similar e-mails from coworkers, family, or friends.

Like a human virus that can spread rapidly from one person to another, revenge should come with the same warning: Do not open! A computer virus travels from one computer to the next causing major destruction. Once it is registered on a computer, it automatically picks up certain codes that sift through our files to destroy all of our personal data. Or it can actually sit on your computer for days before it releases itself (waiting for a certain date) to spread to other computers causing untold damage.

I believe that these three dance steps—*retreat*, *revenge*, and *rehearse*—act like a deadly virus in our lives if we leave them untreated. They spread an epidemic of unforgiveness, a most deadly emotion. Whenever we are injured, we have the option to forgive the offender. We often choose instead to retreat, plan revenge, or continually rehearse the offense. However, we are ultimately destroyed, not the offender.

If we persist in dancing the two movements of *dwell* and *tell*, our injured relationship just gets worse. The offender remains out of our lives forever, and we become a person obsessed with anger, bitterness, and hatred, who passed on the chance to repair an injured relationship when it was offered. Even if reconciliation isn't offered, we can heal ourselves if we simply quit dancing those doubly painful steps.

We have all been hurt and devastated by someone close to us, but we have the option to choose the dance to forgiveness. As Tyler Perry teaches, we can either choose to turn our back on the future or forgive—and walk boldly toward it. If we choose to forgive, do we just let those who hurt us back into our lives without first earning our trust? Absolutely not! In every case, this has to be a decision between the two individuals involved.

In order to prevent dangerous viruses from infecting our computers and causing permanent damage, companies have created anti-virus software, an option that is now available and protects our computers. Like anti-virus software, forgiveness is the only remedy for our own physical, emotional, and spiritual health.

No matter how difficult an injury is, choose to dance to forgiveness. Forgive the person who hurt you, the words that were spoken over you, the abuse that you may have experienced, the husband or wife who walked out on you, the children who rebelled and didn't appreciate what you did for them. The longer you live in this cycle, the more damage the virus will cause. The sooner you load your own personal anti-virus software, the sooner you can heal yourself.

There is a spiritual principal, an effective antidote that if we choose, will result in freedom. Colossians 3:13 says, "You must make allowance for each other's faults and forgive the person who offends you. Remember, the Lord forgave you, so you must forgive others."

Something to Consider (Ponder)

We need to recognize that often the only person being hurt is us; there's no nobility in making ourselves miserable. There's no reward in resurrecting painful memories and rehearsing the hurt. There is only fresh pain.

Only when we're willing to admit that the *Rehearse* dance step is self-destructive are we ready to start dealing with it. Only when we understand that rehearsing our old hurts is like walking on sharp pebbles will we be ready to stop punishing ourselves.

The decision to turn the other cheek is a difficult one because our head and heart are telling us two different things. How do we get them working together so that we can properly heal? You might consider these questions:

- Am I rehearsing a hurt against someone right now, today, at this moment? Who and for what?

- In what way does dwelling on the hurt and telling everybody what someone did to me add to my life or subtract from my life?

- Does repeating my hurt bring me peace, or does it bring me turmoil? In what ways?

- What are some of the visible signs I can see, touch, and feel from dwelling on and telling my hurts (damaged relationships, too much time alone, feeling shut out)?

- Can I choose to forgive? What are the pros and cons of doing so?

Something to Do (Practice)

Try the "empty chair dialogue technique." Sit alone with an empty chair (about three feet away) and pretend it is occupied by the person who hurt you. Really picture him or her sitting there. Close your eyes, if necessary, to visualize what his or her eyes might be saying to you. Now talk to that person—spouse, relative, other significant person, friend, parent, child, or coworker—who is sitting in that chair.

This exercise stimulates your thinking and highlights your emotions and attitudes about the past and the person who hurt you. For example, it may be your father in the chair. Picture him vividly and then talk to him about how you felt when he was unfaithful to your mother (or whatever he did).

Really pour your heart out and express your feelings: anger, resentment, hatred. Now ask, why did you behave this way? How did you feel when others knew what you had done? Questions are essential. Ask your father: "How could you have done this?" "Why didn't you ever say you were sorry?" "Did it hurt you that your adult children chose to shut you out of their lives and their children's lives?"

Putting yourself in your father's shoes might make you better understand the temptation and reality of the offense. Though not condoning it, you might become more empathetic and understanding and decide it's time to try the dance to forgiveness.

The next step—and this could be a tough one—is to switch places and sit in that chair and reply to your own empty chair. Speak as if you were your father. Then, when you're finished, return to sit in your own chair and talk to your father again. Be prepared for tears, rage, even surprises.

Remember the old shampoo directions: "Lather, rinse, repeat"? Do this exercise, if possible, with each person who has wronged you. If you find it helpful and each time rid yourself of past hurts, repeat until you feel "clean" of the hurts and hopeful about the future.

Or try the "write and burn a letter" technique: Put down everything you feel and ever wanted to say about the hurt caused by someone close to you. Describe your pain, confusion, fear, rage, and despair. Tell of your love or hate, gratitude or disappointment. Put it all down, perhaps over several days or weeks, until the letter is complete. Then tear it into strips and as you burn each one, pray these words from St. Paul's Letter to the Ephesians (4:31–32): "Let all bitterness and wrath and anger and uproar and slander be put away from you, along

> *"Holding onto the past only stands in your way."*
>
> TINA TURNER

with all malice. Be kind to one another, tender-hearted, forgiving each other, just as God has forgiven you."

Remember, it is yourself you are forgiving here. Remember how long you have abused yourself through holding onto this betrayal, this pain, this anger, hurt, frustration, and even fear. Forgiveness is a drain being pulled from a tub full of brackish water. Every inch that recedes gives you back the power and control over your own life.

Isn't it time you forgave someone to release yourself?

Something to Say (Prayer)

Compassionate God, I'm coming to you because I need to forgive. I am dealing with feelings of unforgiveness. I have experienced devastating hurts at the hands of another.

I want to forgive him or her for making light of my injuries, for not saying sorry. I don't have anything to bring to you except all this hurt and pain.

I don't want to continue to dwell on what was said and done to me, nor do I want to continually tell it to everyone. I know people are kind and pretend to listen, but they walk away shaking their heads, thinking, "Enough already, forgive."

It's time to throw away the old dancing shoes that only stalled or stopped me from forgiveness. It's time to put on new shoes and dance in them to forgiveness. In Jesus' name, I pray. Amen.

Rethink

Waking Up

"But when he came to his senses, he said, 'How many of my father's hired hands have more than enough bread, but I am dying here with hunger!'"

❧ LUKE 15:17

Forgiving those who have injured us can feel impossible at times. It can be so difficult to release the injury and move forward. Something in us feels violated and robbed.

The offender's actions stole something from us, so we feel justified in holding onto our anger, bitterness, and hatred. We rationalize that they deserve our wrath and deep inside we long for the chance to "pay them back" for what they have done. We want them to suffer. Sometimes we hold onto our bitterness, even after the offending party has sought our forgiveness.

As a hospital chaplain, I am often confronted by families with the question, "When do I let go?" This is a familiar image to anyone who has had a relative in ICU—an old, dying gentleman, for example. He is hooked up to tubes and his children are gathered around him looking concerned and expressing their love. His eyes are closed, his mouth is open, and a ventilator tube runs down his throat. It is a powerful image.

"When do I let go?" The question could be attached to many issues: loved ones who have passed away; children growing up and getting married; or failure in life or business.

We could make our list very long if we wanted. But let's take a moment and focus on one item that we must let go of: the bitterness of an unforgiving heart.

Something to Learn (Path)

The story is told of a stubborn old farmer who was plowing his field with his mule. A neighbor watched as the farmer tried unsuccessfully to guide the mule by jerking and pulling on the reins without saying a word. Finally, the neighbor said, "I don't want to butt in, but you could save yourself a lot of work if you'd just say, 'Gee-haw' and 'Gitty-up' every now and again." The old-timer mopped his brow and replied, "Yep, I know; but this here mule kicked me six years ago, and I ain't spoke to him since!"

How often have we punished ourselves, all in the name of not forgiving someone else? Unfortunately, the old-timer's response to his mule seems to be the American way. We would rather take the long road of pain and misery and revenge to avoid the straight path to forgiveness. Bottom line, forgiveness isn't always considered a noble characteristic in our society. The desire to withhold forgiveness or "get even" seems more desirable than simply letting things go.

Check out the lyrics from the song "We Bury the Hatchet," by country music star Garth Brooks, especially these two lines:

When it comes to forgettin' baby, there ain't no doubt.
We bury the hatchet but leave the handle stickin' out.

Unforgiveness is not reserved solely for mule farmers. The story is told of two monks who had gone on a day's journey, and the weather became very nasty. On the way home that evening, they had to cross a flooded stream where a woman who needed help to get to the other side was waiting. Seeing her dilemma, one of the monks picked her up and carried her across.

Later that evening the monk who didn't help the woman condemned the one who did, saying, "You were wrong this afternoon helping that lady. You know that in our order we are to have no dealings with the opposite sex." To which the other monk replied, "I carried her only across the stream. You are carrying her still." How often do we let past wounds fester until we are covered with scars that never heal and break relationships that patience and forgiveness might have salvaged?

We can't always avoid injuries in our relationships, but we *can* keep them from creating a great rift of emotional distance between ourselves and our offenders. In fact, once we decide to let go and dance on to forgiveness, many of these relationships become stronger.

Such is the truth of unforgiveness: Not only does it ruin bonds, but it breaks those who could have become stronger through reconciliation. Saint Paul's words to the Philippians speak to this very issue: "Forgetting those things which are behind...I press on toward the goal" (Philippians 3:13).

Unforgiveness chains us to the hurt; like the old farmer with the mule we'll gladly make our own lives harder if we perceive that we're somehow "getting back" at the offender. Whatever stage of life or development we were in when the hurt occurred, becomes the state we still live in.

This is true both physically and emotionally. If our spouse leaves us, we're likely to leave our bedroom exactly the way it was when we were married; all the better to surround ourselves with the pain we're addicted to. If we're hurt in our teens and never get over it, we're still emotionally teenagers when it comes to relationships. We cannot move on to the next dance step until we let unforgiveness go!

"Father forgive them." These were among Jesus' last human words. They must be our first if we are to get on with living and quit letting the past wrongs in our lives destroy us. It's not easy to forgive. It is a commitment we must risk. The decision to dance to forgiveness is a healthy choice. Unforgiveness only takes its toll on us by becoming a *drain*, a *strain*, and a *pain*.

A Drain: I'm So Tired

When we refuse to forgive we are wasting valuable time and needed energy. Unforgiveness requires heavy maintenance. To stay angry and bitter we have to be at the top of our game to avoid any misstep lest we smile, acknowledge, or, heaven forbid, forgive.

I've had people over my years of ministry tell me that they are *tired all the time*. They feel drained of strength, literally on the verge of sleep no matter the time of day or night. After speaking with these people, I've learned that they still have a list of people they refuse to forgive. There's no physical illness afflicting them; they simply need to let go of what has drained them, refill their empty lives with happiness and forgiveness.

When we choose the dance step, *Rethink*, we finally come to an awareness that the only way to replenish ourselves physically, emotionally, and spiritually is to readily and freely forgive as the Father through Christ Jesus has forgiven us. We'll find more than just peace of mind when we choose the dance to forgiveness; we'll discover heaven's smile, soundness of mind, and renewed physical strength as well.

There's a lot of wisdom in Ephesians: "Be angry, and do not sin: do not let the sun go down on your wrath" (4:26). It's okay to be angry, it's only natural, but don't dwell on it more than a few hours. Each day we should clear our minds and emotions of the injuries caused by others before we go to sleep. This will prevent us from tossing and turning in the middle of the night, and we will wake up refreshed.

A Strain: I'm Making Others Miserable

Our unforgiving attitude affects everyone in our circle of family and friends. We put them in awkward situations, especially if they get along with the person who has injured us. In some ways we say, "Draw the line in the sand and decide whose side you're on!" We pin their backs against the wall and say, "Choose!"

Think of the pain divorced parents inflict on their children when they degrade or deride the ex-spouse in front of or even directly to the children. It's hard enough growing up these days, but with the added pressure of hearing what a "cheat" your father is or what a "flake" your mother is, it gets even worse.

Our adult relationships suffer as well. When we make things unpleasant for our mutual friends by gossiping vengefully about another mutual friend, we sacrifice yet another friendship. How often do we think our friends will stick around to hear our bitterness before fleeing to the person we're so bitter about?

The insatiable habits of unforgiveness, ultimatums and "choosing sides" forces family and friends to walk on eggshells, being careful not to pay too much attention to the offender. Parties and celebrations become a strain for everyone, particularly if other family members and friends have actually chosen sides in the conflict (and it's not your side).

In addition to ultimatums, we issue elaborate warnings: "If I come to the party and so and so is there, don't expect me to talk to him. You know what he did to me." Or we offer excuses thinly veiled as threats: "Thanks for the invitation to the graduation, but I hear you also invited my ex-wife so I'm not coming. I can't stand to be in the same room with her and breathe the same air." And finally, "I know you have to invite him to the school play, he's the kids' grandfather, I get that, but don't you dare sit him anywhere near me." It becomes a no-win situation for everyone involved.

I've had several occasions where an ex-spouse refused to sit next to their ex at their son's or daughter's wedding. If any of you have been involved in the planning of a wedding, you know the many hours of silent toil spent figuring out guest lists and seating charts to avoid this type of slight. I had to tell them at the rehearsal, in not so many words, "Grow up, stop making it about you—it's your son's or daughter's day, not yours. If you make a scene at this wedding, your son or daughter will remember it for the rest of his or her life."

A Pain: I'm Hurting Others

Unforgiveness is like a toothache that never goes away. The nerve is always exposed, ever waiting for that person or situation that like a cold drink hits the raw nerve of unforgiveness. Many people will go to their graves with unresolved hurts; they carry their pain that far. When we are in pain over what was said or done to us, we become a pain and hurt to others as well.

We lose our patience with friends, fly off the handle at work, or lash out at family members, all because we have the wound exposed and are too afraid—or too stubborn—to sit in the dentist's chair and have the damage repaired.

We interpret every word spoken to us through the prism of our hurt; there is no room for clarity, sensitivity, or objectivity through this haze of pain. I have been in situations with people in which there was a gross overreaction to a word someone spoke or an action that was taken. Although I was shocked and thought this reaction came "out of left field," it was really the person responding to years of hurt that spilled over in unlikely situations.

It's like the bucket you put under a leak and then forget about; eventually it's going to overflow and spill all over the floor and it only takes one single drop to tip the scales. It's this "last drop" that often turns on the floodgates of emotion, even though it's the few million drops beforehand that actually cause the problem. But who will be around to bear the burden of our "spillover"? Usually it's not the person we're so mad at, but a friend, colleague, or family member. By holding onto our hurt and not letting go, we often alienate those people closest to us (and the ones we need the most) with our self-destructive behavior. As a result, we risk losing the contacts we need the most at this point in our lives.

Eventually, most hurting people do wake up and say to themselves, "It's time to do something about the relationship. My behavior is out of control. I let it go on far too long. I've slammed the door in their faces one too many times and slapped the hands offered in forgiveness way too often. I can't go on like this, because now my hurt is hurting others."

When we're hurting someone else, we're acting from a place of hurt. No longer are we simply being selfish or even naïve; we're being hurtful, and no matter how much we hurt, few of us actively seek to hurt others—particularly those we care about the most (and tend to lash out at the most). To avoid slipping into this dance we need to diminish the hurt to make room for forgiveness. Instead of being hurting people who hurt others, we then become forgiving people who are forgiving others.

When you're ready to stop hurting and begin forgiving, start by saying the Prayer of Jabez: "Oh that you would bless me indeed and enlarge my border, and that your hand might be with me, and that you would keep me from harm that it may not pain me!" (1 Chronicles 4:10). And God granted Jabez what he requested. Ask God to give us the power to go through the hurt, to open our eyes to see beyond ourselves, and to forgive without causing hurt to anyone else.

Take the Lead

My all-time favorite parable of Jesus is the prodigal son (Luke 15:11–32). In this remarkably heartwarming story, the younger son wanted to enjoy life and "spread his wings." He could not wait to get away and indulge in reckless behavior. He was having "the time of his life"—that is, until the money ran out. Then the younger son "came to himself." He woke up. He took off his blinders, became aware of his inappropriate behavior, and decided to go home and reconcile with his father.

How humbling this must have been; the long return to the homestead he had abandoned in favor of "the good life." He must have rehearsed his speech of reconciliation over and over as he walked home. We can only image the stunned look on his face when his father came running toward him instead of denying him, as he had every right to expect. Instead of stern reproach, he received only joy, forgiveness, and love. We have the hurting father forgiving the hurtful son; no emotional baggage, no emotional outburst, no vengeance.

Like the prodigal son's forgiving father, we too must muster the desire and determination to restore a valued relationship by being persistent in our dance to forgiveness. It's the only way we'll return to normalcy and preserve that relationship. The person who has hurt us cannot unsay or undo what happened, but we *can* decide and we *can* choose to carry it around or leave it and let it go. We have reams of evidence to support why holding onto past hurts is harmful and just as much proof that letting go leads to instant and irrevocable healing.

Making the right decision allows *us* to reign in our lives, not anger, bitterness, hatred, or revenge. It allows us to give people who have injured us the benefit of the doubt that they are sincere when they say, "I'm sorry." (Why shouldn't we believe them?) Forgiveness encourages us to offer them another chance at making things right and gives us the opportunity to regain a friendship, a spouse, a family member.

Something to Consider (Ponder)

The 2002 movie *Changing Lanes* sets off a brutal cycle of revenge between two men who began this story, on Good Friday no less, as complete strangers. A traffic accident brings them together, and they are very much alike in temperament. Both have problems with life. Doyle Gipson (Samuel L. Jackson) is a recovering alcoholic on the brink of losing his family forever, and he is determined not to let this happen. He has one serious hurdle on his horizon: Gavin Banek.

Banek (Ben Affleck) is on a power trip in a career fast lane. When the two collide on an interstate highway in busy New York traffic, Gavin not only refuses to provide his insurance card, he refuses to give Doyle a ride to court where there's a hearing about visitation for his children. Gavin is in a hurry to a court case of his own, and he accidentally drops an important file that he *must have* to win a case that is critical to his law firm.

Doyle, therefore, is late for *his* court appearance, and not only loses visitation, his ex-wife announces she's moving to the other coast so Doyle will never see his children again. In another court room, Gavin lies about his lost file and must find Doyle to get it back—without an address. Gavin, a partner in his father-in-law's firm, begins to realize just how important that file is to the firm, and wonders why. He comes face to face with the reality that he's an unwitting pawn used to trick clients to make the law firm wealthier. He looks at what he is becoming and is not pleased.

Unable to get Doyle to give him the file, Gavin tries to destroy Doyle's life even further until he gives it back. But Doyle, feeling the pain of Gavin's onslaught, strikes back. Both men actually *want* to do the right thing, but they keep making wrong choices.

This movie makes us ask:

- What's the right thing to do when someone causes us injury?

- Does being powerful mean never having to say you're sorry?

- Is saying "sorry" enough to make up for ruining someone's life?

- Once you begin ruining someone's life, where do you stop...or do you ever stop?

> *"Hanging onto resentment is letting someone you despise live rent-free in your head."*
>
> ANN LANDERS

While watching this film I was struck by how easily avoidable both of these men's predicaments were. Just a few simple choices in the right direction, and all the pain and hurt could have been avoided. And yet, time and time again, both characters consistently choose to hurt one another.

As you consider which dance step you want to take next, also think about and talk about these questions:

- How can I really love someone who is hurtful?

- Should I allow this person to stay in my life or should I shut him or her out to protect myself from further hurt?

Something to Do (Practice)

Have your hurting list of hurtful people handy; it's never too far from your thoughts anyway. Take a ten-inch deflated balloon. For each person on your list, blow a breath of air into the balloon. The more anger you feel, the more air you will blow.

If you keep blowing, what happens? What can you learn from this exercise? What will happen to you if you don't let go of your anger and revenge? How long before pent-up anger and unforgiveness makes you "pop" for good?

Something to Say (Prayer)

Gentle God, please help me to be a forgiving person by taking back the reins of my life and refusing to allow anger, bitterness, hatred, and revenge to control me.

When Jesus was hurt again and again by those he loved, he continued to pursue them, love them, and seek the best for them. I need to take Jesus seriously when it comes to giving those who hurt me another chance. I do not want people to know me as an unforgiving person.

Specifically I ask you to help me fully forgive (Name). I need to get all of these hurts off my chest; I need to forgive whomever has hurt me and then let it go.

Good and faithful God, help me to choose forgiveness in my embattled relationships. I know it is difficult to forgive others who have injured my life and caused me hurt, but it is the only way for me to have peace; sweet peace. In Jesus' name I pray. Amen.

❧ STEP 6 ❧

Respond
Loving Confrontation

"You will know the truth, and the truth will set you free."   ❧ JOHN 8:32

Very few of us welcome confrontation. To tell a coworker we're unhappy with his or her performance, to tell someone we're dating we're "just not that into them anymore," to tell a friend he's gained weight, or a sister she's not living up to her potential, well, these things can get painful, sticky, and downright unpleasant.

Now more than ever, it's easier to send an e-mail or text message to let someone know we're unhappy. It's much more difficult to actually pick up the phone, let alone confront him or her in person. But some confrontations aren't just necessary, they're healthy, as we'll see in this next dance step: *Respond.*

Something to Learn (Path)

I stood by Bruce's side in the emergency room the night they

84

fought to save his son's life. Frank had tried to kill himself with an overdose of sleeping pills. When he finally woke up, Frank felt angry and didn't want to live any longer. Besides the emotional pain and the physical discomfort he felt, there was something else: Frank didn't want to see his father. In fact, he hated him and wanted Bruce out of his life completely.

Their last fight had sent him over the edge. Bruce has three children, including Frank. Frank always wore the label given to him by his father as "different." As a child, he had been weak and delicate. With the innocent cruelty of children, Frank's playmates had continually aggravated the stunted, skinny boy to tears. In high school, Frank was so small that he was always being mistaken for someone's little brother.

After high school Frank studied art. He now works for an Internet company designing web pages. A few of his works have even gained national recognition. He was always a reserved individual who stuffed his feelings inside and kept them hidden. This night, however, his father got the best of him and the hurt became unbearable.

Bruce realized what he had almost lost. In an attempt to reconcile with his son, he sat by his bedside, took his hand, and asked for his forgiveness: "Frank," he confessed, "I've been wrong for the way I have hurt you. Please forgive me. I've treated you just like my father treated me, and I hated him. Please give me another chance."

Few of us make it through life without being hurt by others. When it happens, our feelings can be overwhelming. At first, we may feel anger and bitterness. Justice isn't just what we want; it's what we feel we deserve. And, while we're at it, we want the other person to hurt, too.

Do we get over it or get even? Will we heal from the experience or continue to hate? Letting go is not easy, but it's the only way to stop punishing ourselves and having our hearts remained locked in resentment. To continue to hold on and embrace revenge toward another, to cling to old hurts that we just can't let go of, means we are chained to that person by an emotional link that is stronger than steel. Forgiveness is the only way to break free and reclaim a life that is rightfully our own.

Sadly, Frank and Bruce's case is as extreme as you might imagine; live with pain and hurt long enough, bury it far enough, and eventually it will breed and multiply and fester and plot until, when you least expect it, it will drown you in pain and sorrow. Sometimes, as in Frank's case, death seems preferable to living another moment with the agony of old hurts.

Often, the hardest thing to do in a relationship is to let the other person know that they hurt us. When we're hurt, it can be hard to find the words to express our feelings; our instinct to avoid confrontation puts us at odds with opening up and sharing how we truly feel.

If we do confront, it is often from the heart and not the head; we say and do things out of rage and betrayal. We overreact, throw tantrums, break down, or even become physical. Often, in our anger, we can make the situation worse for both parties.

It doesn't need to be this way.

Most of us find it hard to express our feelings, because voicing what we feel is difficult, especially when great emotion is involved. When we try to say what we want to say, we end up being tongue-tied, misunderstood, or worse, end up saying the wrong thing. So instead of risking humiliation or rejection, we keep everything to ourselves, shut out and shut down, and allow the hurt to fester.

Think about the people who have caused us injury and left us hurting. Often we sweep the feelings under the carpet and act as if they don't exist, or deny the fact that something awful happened to us in the first place: "It wasn't so bad." "It happened a long time ago." "Really? I barely remember that happening."

But regardless of the lies we tell ourselves and others, what happened happened; saying it didn't, burying the hurt or denying its existence doesn't make it go away. The feelings we resist will come out in unhealthy ways and impossible-to-scale walls stay in place. Avoidance of the person continues, silent treatment is ongoing, replaying and rehashing of what happened perpetuates, and allies are still being recruited to "see it our way."

If we're harboring anger, bitterness, and hatred, eventually they will have us under control. Our hurt will come out in other ways and undermine our relationships anyway. Eventually that "flashover" moment of emotion will overwhelm us. To dance to forgiveness, we need to get everything out in the open and clear the dance floor of all that hurt and pain. It's been buried long enough. We need to give ourselves the go-ahead to dig it all out, deal with it, and put it behind us.

Dance step six, *Respond*, teaches how to bring our feelings into loving confrontation. Why loving confrontation? It's important we don't confront from our anger, which will leave a permanent scar and stands little chance of healing the relationship.

When we arrive at this dance step we are well on our way to being released from all the anger, bitterness, and hatred others have caused us. I know it can seem unpleasant; finally facing the person who wronged you, whether recently or many years ago. Like Bruce and Frank, the reunion can bring up old hurts and fresh pain. But look what it took to get father and son together in that case; don't let the feelings go on so long that suicide seems a more pleasant option than confrontation!

Learning to face others really isn't about them so much as it is about ourselves; as it is about responding to the hurt and pain with maturity, objectivity, and the knowledge that by having this reunion both parties can move forward and live their lives in peace.

Gene's Got the Moves

It's never easy to look someone directly in the eyes and say a difficult truth such as, "I feel you betrayed my trust." The need for loving confrontation is urgent, no matter the difficulty involved in setting up or planning for such a reunion. As we have seen, unresolved injuries in our relationships can result in the breakdown of mutual trust and the breeding of fear and avoidance. A willingness to be lovingly truthful with someone who has hurt us takes the wisdom to know when to speak and when to keep quiet, as well as the courage to face the outcome of the confrontation. Sometimes all of our best efforts to show love and reconciliation are met with verbal expressions of anger, denial, and avoidance.

I recall counseling sessions with Gene. In those sessions we talked about his life and the hurt he carries caused by his father, whom he hasn't forgiven. From these sessions, we can see the value of responding to hurts with loving confrontation.

"It takes me two days to get emotionally ready when I go and visit my father," said Gene, "and then another day to get a clear head again from his comments and criticisms. I have so much anger and bitterness in my heart for him, and I don't know how I can ever forgive him!"

Gene was clearly at odds with his father, but despite the fact that both were grown men, these hurts looked to be sticking around for a long time. "My father, whom I am named after, always knows what to say to hurt me and he leaves me feeling bad about myself. My mother is gentle and kind and often acts like a buffer, trying to turn my dad's sarcasm into a joke or a positive statement, but it hurts; it really hurts."

Gene related to me that years earlier he'd decided not to follow in his father's footsteps and take over the family bakery. "I wanted to be independent. I went to school and completed my degree in elementary education. I married Cathy, whom I met in college. We both teach in the same school district in Ohio and we love it."

Reading between the lines, it seemed to me that Gene's father had never forgiven him for "deserting" the family bakery and branching out on his own, despite the younger Gene's obvious success and happiness.

"He deflates me by throwing sarcastic remarks at me," Gene confessed, "and makes me want to start screaming and yelling." Although his father is clearly not helping things, it is Gene who needs to manage what he is allowing his father to do to him. If he ever wants true independence, Gene needs to step back, calm down, and take a long look at what he needs to do.

Gene thinks his dad is carrying around a belly-full of anger. And his anger is only covering his disappointment that Gene isn't working by his side in the bakery. Just as Gene needs to forgive his dad for his comments, his dad needs to forgive Gene for choosing his own career.

Clearly, this conflict has been simmering too long and is threatening to "boil over" at any moment—unless Gene takes steps now to avoid this flashover point by having a loving confrontation with his father. Gene needs to finish this business and bring it to a close once and forever. It has festered and is creating distance in the relationship, causing more harm than good.

Together, we selected "loving confrontation" to repair his relationship with his father. When I mentioned the words to Gene, I could sense he felt uncomfortable. I told him it's normal to feel uneasy, but this was no idle choice; if he really wanted to get the point across to his father, it needed to be face-to-face.

Confrontation usually conjures up negativity and unpleasantness. Some think confrontation is unhealthy, if only because their negative connotations are so strong, but it's not. It's okay to rock the boat, ruffle some feathers, and make waves. More importantly, it's our right to be okay with who we are, what we do, and how we feel. Why is it okay for Gene's father to say whatever he wants about Gene's life choices, but not okay for Gene to talk back, rationally and thoughtfully, about how *he* feels? We need to bring our hurts out in the open if we really care about each other.

We also discussed how risky it is to confront someone who has created such stress and strain in your life; we talked about the tendency to "flash over" and release a torrent of pent-up anger and frustration. Together we looked at the possible reactions Gene might expect from his father, and these things topped the list: go on the defense, snap back, dismiss Gene as ridiculous, laugh at Gene, go silent and walk away.

So, there are the negatives. But…there's *also* the possibly Gene's father may listen and think about what has been said. It may give his father an opportunity to talk with his son, get everything out in the open, repair the hurt, and move on from there. Even if all Gene does is plant the seed in his father's head, better late than never.

"My father always shoots from the lip. He's not careful with his words," Gene said. "Many of his friends label him 'Quick-draw Eugene.' That's something I've experienced. So I need to get myself prepared for a possible verbal attack. But it's now or never! I can't let him continue to set me off and drive me crazy with his comments."

I continued to encourage Gene not to let this slide. He has been putting up with his father's behavior far too long. His feelings have been hurt and the time is ripe to dance to forgiveness. A month after this conversation, Gene called for an appointment. He seemed excited, uplifted, and anxious. After we agreed on a day and time to meet, I felt he must have confronted his father.

He did confront his dad, and he felt relieved and reconciled. "I put it to him," Gene admitted. "Before I did, I prepared myself. Since I know he likes to interrupt and never let me finish a sentence, I decided to bring an egg timer along."

"An egg timer?" I asked.

"Yes. Since my father's a baker, he knows the importance of timing with baking. I thought the egg timer would be a good way to control the conversation by giving each of us a chance to talk and listen to each other without jumping into the conversation before we'd finished expressing our thoughts and feelings."

Great idea!

Gene went to visit his father on a Sunday afternoon. He expressed his need to talk. Immediately his father jumped in and asked, "Talk about what? Do you need money?"

Then Gene set ground rules for their conversation. He asked his father not to respond until he was finished. His dad chuckled when Gene showed him the egg timer. Gene further explained why he brought it along: "Dad, you can't say a word until it's your turn. The egg timer will be like a time clock. Once the sand is all on the one side, it will be your turn to respond to me."

Gene's dad asked him, somewhat pragmatically, I thought, "Well, what if I need more time?" Gene assured him he would give him all the time he needed because what they were going to talk about was important to their relationship—no matter how long it took!

Gene then shared with me how he expressed his gratitude to his father. "My dad worked long and hard without ever complaining. There was always plenty of food on the table, enough clothing, and 'extras' that others in our neighborhood didn't have. I thanked him and let him know how much I appreciated all he has done for me."

After affirming his dad, Gene then added, "I always felt you were unhappy and dissatisfied with my decision to teach and not become a baker. Too many times your comments about teaching hurt me. I would go home and feel as if I had been through the wringer. Your words would stick in my mind for days. Dad, I need this to change. I want to visit you and not leave feeling this way anymore."

"Well, Gene," his father confessed, "I *am* disappointed in you. I wanted you to step in, learn from me, and then give you a well-established business. It was my dream to add to the sign outside the bakery two words: 'and son.' You had different plans that I didn't like. I wanted you to be happy."

"Dad," Gene explained, "I'm happy teaching. I love doing what I'm doing. Every night before I go to bed, I ask myself how I have made a difference in one student's life today."

"I'm sure you're making a difference in their lives," his dad said. "You're talented, and kids would warm up to you and feel safe around you. I can see now that I let my stubbornness and anger cloud my vision, making it impossible for me to see you grow in your own dream. I let my own agenda for you get in the way of our relationship. And my mouth has gotten me into trouble."

Gene's father paused, and then continued, "Your mother always says I speak without knowing my brain and mouth are connected. These are feelings I've kept inside too long. I am so sorry I've not been truthful with you and always hurt you. Gene, it would kill me inside if you stopped coming to see me."

Gene told me this was the first time he had ever seen this side of his father: emotional, contrite, open, and honest. The conversation continued and together both men felt relieved that everything was out in the open. He and his father agreed to keep talking and his father asked him to remind him when he crosses the line with hurtful words.

The ice has been broken, the wall has tumbled down, and now they can come together in mutual respect and appreciation. Gene admitted it was a good start, but he knew there was still work to be done if he was ever to undo the many hurts and slights of the past. But he also admitted his own culpability in not confronting his father sooner; now both men need to continue being truthful with each other and express their feelings when words hurt their relationship.

There's no guarantee his father will not say hurtful things again, but the difference is that now everything is out in the open and managed: behavior, motives, and feelings. Gene and his father have taken their relationship to a deeper level and are talking soul to soul. By selecting loving confrontation, Gene finally felt good inside and will feel free to share his real, genuine, authentic self with his dad whenever the need arises.

Because Gene cared so much about his relationship with his father (and didn't want to give up on it), he knew that he needed to confront him by speaking the truth in love. When they sat down in mutual love and respect and talked over the issues and problems in their relationships, buried feelings surfaced but...both men were mature enough to face them, work through them, and appear on the other side stronger and more sensitive. It provided father and son with a rare opportunity to raise their concerns, express their feelings, and work together to resolve them.

Just Copy It

There's no need to reinvent the wheel when it comes to loving confrontation. We can just follow Gene's game plan: choose the time and the place carefully, with no disturbance; think about what we're going to say and how we'll say it; don't apologize for the hurt or water it down; ask what you need from the other person and then listen to his or her response.

The most important part is getting over the fear or hesitancy and committing to the confrontation. Yes, it can seem unpleasant, yes, there are 1,001 excuses you could make for why this isn't "the right time" to do it, but just think what Gene's life would be like if he hadn't made the time, set the ground rules, bitten the bullet, sat down with his dad, and hashed out these issues. He would still be the fearful, bitter, and basically fatherless man he'd been for so long. Now he was, quite literally, a happy man; and all because he made the commitment to a loving confrontation and stuck to it.

Never see confrontation as a battleground, but as a better

> *"Hurt is inevitable. But, how we evade it, how we give in to it, and how we confront it, is our choice."*

UNKNOWN

ground for healing a hurting relationship. Loving confrontation is gospel-rooted. Jesus said that if a neighbor wrongs us, don't avoid the issue, but speak with that person face-to-face (Matthew 18:15–17). The hope is to clear the air and make things right before it's too late and before the small slight becomes a big one that takes forever to untangle.

This is one of the hardest things to do—to lovingly confront someone who has hurt us. Jesus is not a wound-opener, but a wound-mender. Jesus knows something we are still learning: harboring resentment, holding a grudge, and trying to get even *only hurts us*. We simply need to ask Jesus to give us the courage and the confidence, the desire and the determination to say, "No more!"

Something to Consider (Ponder)

By keeping our hurts in cold storage we only fill our hearts with bitterness and build silent, stony walls of hatred between those we love and those who love us. It's vital that our lives be knit together with a continuous outpouring of loving confrontation, no matter how daunting that task might seem at first.

Buried revenge, hidden doubts, and covered-up wounds leave little hope for intimacy. Don't ignore. Pour. Spill out the truth about what has hurt! Why should we ignore the injuries in our lives and go on with life as usual?

Something to Do (Practice)

God uses difficult situations to mature us and heal us. Read St. Paul's advice to the Ephesians: "Speaking the truth in love, we are to grow up" (4:15). Burn this into your memory, copy it into your day planner, stick it to your fridge or your bathroom mirror where you'll see it every day.

Consider it as your only motivation for confrontation.

Something to Say (Prayer)

Loving God, I was hurt. It wasn't my fault. It swept me off my feet and took me someplace far from where I intended to go. I want to forgive, but I need you to help me get up and back on my feet so I can dance to forgiveness.

Where there is a broken or strained relationship in my life and distance between me and any other family member or friend because of unforgiveness, I want to respond by speaking the truth in love and breaking down that wall.

It all starts with one step: loving confrontation. It's the only way I can tell the person who hurt me how I feel. I need to do this before these feelings get the best of me. I know it's a daring dance step, but the only one that really works.

Compassionate God, you know what I go through when people hurt me. I want to grow in trust again, and with your help I will. Give me an extra helping of courage to do this. In Jesus' name, I pray. Amen.

Reminder

Setting Boundaries

"In everything, therefore, treat people the same way
you want them to treat you."   ❧ MATTHEW 7:12

Admitting that we're wrong can be challenging for most
people. It's human nature, it seems, to avoid admitting our
wrongdoings. We don't confess to our own sins, but we're more
than quick to point at the errors of someone else's ways.

"So I snapped at you, but you made me do it with your
incessant nagging!"

"It's not my fault I insulted your family, and what were you
doing inviting them over again so soon?"

"Why wouldn't I snap? If you had a 'real' job, you'd snap,
too!"

We can't just admit our guilt and take the consequences, we
have to take the other person down a peg or two while we're at
it! A dance school is full of mirrors and that's because mirrors

are a dancer's ally, letting him or her know what the moves look like to observers. In our dance to forgiveness we, too, must take a long, hard look in the mirror and accept personal responsibility for our actions. Maybe we are the victim, here, but that doesn't mean we've acted blamelessly in our acting out, moody, or emotional behavior. This next dance step is about looking inward and healing openly and honestly. We start this step by reminding ourselves that the feelings of others count as much as our own.

Something to Learn (Path)

Jerome was upset with his wife's spending habits.

"I waited for her to come home," he said one day, "and went ballistic on her, reducing her to tears. She didn't deserve that." Regardless of the pain Jerome obviously caused his wife, he's being accountable for his own actions. The more we try to cover up or justify the injury we've caused, the more determined everyone will be to prove us wrong. If we hurt someone, the only words we need to say are "Mea culpa" or in more modern parlance, "My bad" (my fault or my mistake). I kind of like this expression because after all it was our "bad"; we did do something wrong. Why not fess up to it and face the issue head on? If we caused the hurt, it's time to step up to the plate and accept what we said or did, be accountable and avoid adding anything hurtful, judgmental, or recriminatory to our apology. We have to learn that it's not imperative that we force the other person to feel worse just because we're apologizing, that we don't have to take anyone down with us if we've made a mistake and have to fess up.

Being cool takes ten magical words, the most important words we can say to someone we've hurt: "I'm sorry. I made a mistake. Please forgive me." No single phrase can strengthen a relationship more securely than the ability to admit our wrongdoing and offer the hope of reconciliation. It's refreshing and disarming, honest and frequently unexpected.

In our hurtful haze it's easy to forget the feelings of the injured party. The look on the face of someone we love, a single tear-drop, or a slammed door can snap us back into focus and make us realize how rash and hurtful we've been. By then, of course, it's often too late; we justify our actions via the other person's behavior and convince ourselves we were "in the right" for what we said. But "feeling right" won't heal the wounds of harsh words, and if they're not countered quickly, those wounds can fester; just like our unforgiveness.

Jerome said to his wife, "Janet, we need to talk." They decided that after work they would sit down and clear the air. They began by turning off their cell phones so they wouldn't be interrupted, and they sat close to each other. Jerome began by taking ownership for his horrible behavior. "Janet, our relation-ship means too much to me. You're the most important person in my life. I'm so sorry I hurt your feelings, please forgive me. I don't have any explanation for my behavior. I will try my best to never explode on you again."

This was a good apology for Jerome. He didn't say, "I'm sorry if I hurt your feelings, but you backed me into a corner with your shopping." Or "I apologize for what I said, but you spent money we don't have and drove me to it." He took owner-ship for what he said by avoiding "if" or "but" statements that would have turned the tables back on his wife in a judgmental or blaming manner. Such statements weaken our apology and give more pain to an already injured person.

Janet then responded, "Thank you for not lecturing me about financial responsibility. I admire that you didn't even bring up my spending this time. You care about my feelings. That means so much to me. When you exploded I became fright-ened. Thank you for promising not to do it again. I promise to be more responsible with our money."

Since we want to be authentic ourselves, we need to have authenticity in our relationships. We can't keep sweeping things under the carpet, expecting them to magically disappear just because they're out of sight or put on hold. Neglecting, denying, avoiding, ignoring, or running away from our offenders results in stagnant, distant, cold, and disconnected relationships—in other words, relationships headed for certain death. Our feelings will sneak out through nasty digs and they will damage others.

Dance step seven, *Reminder*, highlights the interaction between the hurting and the hurtful. This interaction is elegantly choreographed in three graceful reminder-movements: *I value you...I need you...I want you.*

I value you. We have been hurt, sometimes deeply, but the relationship means too much to us to allow these feelings of anger, bitterness, and hatred to separate us. Our initial approach to our hurt is essential. When we approach our hurt from a place of caring about the other, our words will be softer and our message more clearly heard. If we respond to the hurt by being selfish or indulgent, it will be reflected in our harsh words or even simply a harsh tone.

The hurt may have derailed our relationship, but we need to get it back on track before it's too late. Our relationship with the one who injured us has tremendous value and if we don't share how important this person is to us, well, how will they ever know it?

I need you. When we've been hurt, all we want to know is the reason why the hurtful action or words were directed at us. Many times we say to ourselves: "I didn't deserve to be treated that way by you." Or, "I thought we were good friends, but how could someone do this to a good friend?" It's time to inquire, and not pour salt on our emotional wounds, but rather to ask, "What happened?"

It all starts by saying, "We need to talk." Then, "I need you to listen. I respect you and want your respect. Recently something you said or something you did has hurt me and has gotten in our way. I want you to know how I feel about it." Then we share what we've been carrying inside, openly and honestly, with no time limits, hidden agendas, or deadlines.

It's important to tweak our listening skills by focusing on the other. When having this conversation, try to understand and not judge, blame, advise, or interrupt. Repeat back the things we heard to avoid misunderstanding.

We need to listen and share our understanding of the event(s) and what took place. Our offenders need to walk in our shoes for a few moments and see the world through our eyes; to understand what they did to us. They can't assume they know how we feel or think, by shaking their head and waving their hands in the air saying, "Yeah, yeah, I know what you're feeling or what you're thinking I said, but…"

Remember, this is about relationships and relationships exist between two people. So after we get everything said that's important to us, we need to walk in the other's shoes. It's their turn to speak and our turn to listen so we can try and understand what motivated their behavior to treat us the way they did. Talking about it and listening closely is healthy and it mends our hurting hearts more quickly.

I want you. It's at this time we say to the person who injured us, "I really want you to hear my feelings." It's a sacred privilege to have access to our most private and vulnerable feelings.

Many people are reluctant to talk about their feelings because they become a throwback to the injury and a re-living of the hurt. Sometimes it seems easier to deny our feelings, sit on them, or push them back down, but in the long run they fester underneath the surface, only causing us more pain and actually prolonging our hurt. It's time to bring them out of hiding and express them. Only a setting of trust and emotional security can allow us to divulge our deepest, darkest hurts, so this step is vitally important.

No Trespassing

"I'm the best thing that ever happened to you," Alex said regularly to his wife, Molly. "No one else would put up with such a slob." Molly always retaliated by saying, "Look who's calling who a slob. Stop by the mirror and take a long look at yourself!" Needless to say, this couple's relentless verbal battles seriously injured their relationship. Finally, the three of us sat down and looked into ways to bring about healing and change to avoid permanent damage.

I encouraged Alex and Molly to dance through the three graceful reminder-movements: *I value you. I need you. I want you.* They agreed and found them worthwhile and helpful for expressing feelings they had been carrying inside too long. Then we added the final touch: *setting boundaries.*

No dance consists of a single step; every step works together and, in many cases, builds upon the others. So after we work through loving confrontation and have finally danced our graceful reminder-movements, we complete our repertoire by carving deep and strong boundaries to protect ourselves.

Boundaries are our own personal security system, the kind of force field that lets us know that not just anyone can open the front door of our home, walk inside, go to the fridge, grab whatever they want, and plop right down on our couch. When we have such a system in place, we know that if someone tries to steal our car, it's illegal. We know that people are not allowed to access our bank accounts or use our funds for their own purposes, unless we grant consent.

Boundaries as Bridges

A boundary is a space around us that gives us a sense of confidence and safety. Aware of them or not, we all have boundaries, especially physical boundaries: we won't let someone push, punch, kick, or hit us, for example. Unfortunately, we're not so self-protective when it comes to being verbally or emotionally abused; often we're our own worst abusers, putting ourselves down either verbally or mentally before someone else has the chance to do it for us. So we need to establish our "emotional boundaries."

In a healthy relationship, we know who we are and what makes us unique. We have a good sense of our own self-worth. We can think and feel on our own and take responsibility for our thoughts and feelings. Emotional boundaries define who we are and what we value. They establish "what is me" and "what isn't me."

In an unhealthy relationship, we lose that sense of self; it is constantly on guard and frequently tested. Our boundaries slip and fade and become less defined; hence *we* become less defined.

Emotional boundaries are the gates in our invisible fence lines that protect our precious heart and soul. Many people look at boundaries as walls, but when we establish healthy boundaries, they provide a way to distinguish what we choose to let in and let out. They form flexible gates, not stationary walls. It's important after we have been severely hurt to set healthy emotional boundaries so we can make decisions about what is and what isn't acceptable in our relationship(s).

So we have to start looking at boundaries differently; looking at them as good things—as bridges versus barriers. We need to be in charge about who can cross our bridge, or even what messages they can leave.

Our emotional boundaries are meant to protect us and to prohibit people from continuing to "trespass" in our lives and hurt us. Always remember: boundaries are not something that we "set on" another person. Like forgiveness itself, boundaries are about us, what we will and won't accept. We communicate this by saying: "That's all I'm taking from you, I've had enough." The words themselves appear to be drawing a line in the sand.

What a freeing feeling this can be when done correctly, when we respect ourselves enough to prohibit further damage by creating these boundaries. Once our boundaries are firmly in place and enforced, we can finally say: "I forgive you."

Until we draw the line with our emotional boundaries, however, the potential for ongoing hurt is entirely possible and, in some cases, highly probable. Without boundaries, we allow people to treat us as they want to, not as we expect to be treated, in ways convenient for them. If we don't teach people to value us, we have only ourselves to blame when they repeatedly undermine our self-worth and intentionally injure us.

Boundaries prevent present hurt and help us avoid future hurts as well. Remember, forgiveness isn't just about what's happened in the past but learning to avoid transgressions in the future. The boundaries we set today will not only help heal our past but will also provide us with a safe and positive emotional future.

Three Steps to Effective Boundaries

Our boundaries place us in charge of our lives and enable us to hold our ground when people choose to trespass into our lives again and continue hurting us. We communicate through our boundaries how we choose to be treated and what the consequences will be if the hurtful behavior continues.

Without boundaries, there is no clear demarcation line for what is and what isn't acceptable; we flip-flop from one day to the next, being the lovable "punching bag" one day and then the prickly reactionary the next. Boundaries help us be more consistent in our behavior while also telling others what is no longer acceptable. Our boundaries must be clear-cut and they must be enforced, otherwise no one will take them seriously; not even ourselves.

Here's how we can set up our emotional boundaries in three simple steps.

1. *Simply state the problem.* "I want you to know _____." Fill in the blank by describing the hurt you experienced from the person with whom you're establishing the boundary. For example, "I want you to know your words belittle me." Or, "I want you to know the lie you told about me hurt me." Or even, "I want you to know that your cheating on me devastated me."

2. *Make a request.* "I need you to _____." Fill in the blank with what you need and what's absolutely essential to the relationship. You might say something like, "I need you to be more sensitive." Or, "I need you to tell me the truth." "I need you to stop screaming and yelling." "I need you to stop your put-downs." "I need you to let me know where you are when you don't come home at the usual time."

3. *Be firm.* "I insist that _____." Fill in the blank with what is non-negotiable to you in this relationship. You might say something like, "I insist that you stop lying to me." "I insist that you be careful with what I share with you." "I insist that you be faithful to your vows to me."

We often hear of living "a life without limits," but what does that catchy advertising slogan *really* mean? A relationship without limits implies no control-settings, no boundaries, an "anything goes" scenario where we're also *unable* to let people know when they have stepped over the line. In the real world, we set limits through these boundaries. In a sense, they become our no-fly zones and communicate the following must-have caveats in any relationship: "That's as far as you're going." And, "Hurt me once, shame on you. Hurt me again (same incident), shame on me." And finally, "I'm not going to put up with the way you talk to me (or the way you treat me) anymore."

And consequences are always mentioned when you introduce a reasonable boundary. "If you do that again, I will..." Or, "This is the last time you do this to me before I..." Of course, consequences are only as effective as the actions taken to back them up and prove their validity. Don't express a consequence that you're either not going to follow up on or one that you're just not ready for.

Keep On Dancing

Let's face it: No life is pain-free. No matter how authentic or healthy we are, we're still vulnerable to the slings and arrows people constantly send our way. We're human, and humans are vulnerable. But if we are to live as the vulnerable individuals we are, we have to deal with confrontation topped off with well-defined boundaries to complete our dance to forgiveness.

If we do this, we will be well on our way to letting go of our hurtful feelings, repairing our relationships, and turning back to trust. We will be able to reclaim the peace of mind that comes from being truly free. Our vulnerability can actually give us great strength when we acknowledge the fact that we are human beings living in a human world, interacting with other human beings. Once we accept the fact that we will be insulted, injured, and betrayed and are worthwhile nevertheless, we'll find great strength in moving forward with our boundaries toward reconciliation.

The message is clear: we don't have to excuse the injury or approve the awful behavior or deny the hurtful feelings. In fact, we must bravely and totally acknowledge the injury and work through the emotional baggage we have stored away inside. This kind of "emotional workout" gets us in shape as we head down the home stretch in our forgiveness dance marathon. It does take time before we're completely healed, but the nice thing is that we get better every day.

Something to Consider (Ponder)

Denise's husband was very frustrated at work. Alan would come home and yell at her. At first she yelled back, and Alan got angrier and acted even meaner. Denise stuffed her anger down and withdrew from her husband, emotionally and physically. That didn't work either because she was miserable. Regardless of what she did, Alan didn't improve. In her counseling session, I encouraged her to set emotional boundaries for both their sakes.

> *"If you don't have fences [boundaries], any old stray dog can come and walk on your grass."*
>
> RACHELLE DISBENNET-LEE

The following week, Denise told me that she eventually said to Alan in a calm, firm voice, "I am not willing to live this way." To her surprise, Alan changed his attitude and stopped his negative behavior. In fact, he was his kind self again. I imagine that he finally actually "heard" her and realized that he could no longer get away with his actions without some kind of consequence. I applauded Denise for setting a healthy emotional boundary.

For boundaries to be successful, we must be truthful with everyone, including ourselves. When other people's behaviors do not feel good to us, we have to take a stand. "I love you, but I am only willing to stay in this friendship (or relationship) if we can share mutual respect and kindness." This is a healthy way to establish an emotional boundary and avoid another blowout.

You are a good person and you deserve to be treated with love and respect; that's the point of setting boundaries in the first place.

Something to Do (Practice)

Complete the following statements:

People may no longer _____.

I have a right to ask for _____.

To protect myself, it is okay to _____.

Next, finish each sentence with an example of boundaries we can set to honor and respect ourselves.

Something to Say (Prayer)

Understanding God, people have trespassed into my life and are hurting me with their words and actions. I know I can choose to turn my back on them or find ways to get even, but if I make those choices, nothing will be resolved.

Instead I want to be silent with you, collect my feelings, and then courageously confront the one who is causing my hurt.

So I am asking you now for a courageous heart. I want to share my feelings openly and honestly. I also ask for an understanding heart, so I can listen to the other and not to quickly judge or dismiss anything.

I know this sounds so simple and easy, but without your strength behind me, I just can't do it. With you I can take these positive steps to healing and forgiveness. In Jesus' name, I pray. Amen.

❧ STEP 8 ☙

Repair
Patching Up

"Blessed are the peacemakers, for they shall be called children of God." ❧ MATTHEW 5:9

Just like the roofs of our houses, designed to protect and defend us from the elements, our human relationships need to be patched up, repaired, and even "spackled" from time-to-time. This can be a challenge when we're reluctant to forgive, or even confront, leaving potential relationships with gaping holes.

"Spotty" relationships aren't in their natural state. When we're "pushed apart" from people we love and care about, either by a careless word or a thoughtless action, we yearn to put the relationship back together again. We yearn for a resolution to resolve the injuries. We want to repair the gap; it needs to be reconciled. "Reconciliation" comes from the Latin words *re*, meaning "again," and *conciliare*, which means "to bring together," so in the most literal of senses, reconciliation means "to bring together"—or to make friendly—again. And reconciliation is only possible through forgiveness.

Forgiveness is the only way to "patch up" what has been broken through bitter words and unkind actions. It's a necessary dance step moving us from hurt, anger, and brokenness to places of healing, health, and wholeness.

Something to Learn (Path)

Karen and Phyllis have been friends and have worked together for over fifteen years, but about a year and a half ago Phyllis said some unkind things about Karen to a mutual friend and colleague. Naturally Karen was hurt. She felt betrayed. They met to talk about it, but Phyllis didn't acknowledge any wrongdoing, and eventually they cut off contact altogether. Unfortunately, that lack of closure from their final meeting would come back to haunt Karen. *That's that*, Karen thought, *we're finished.*

Somehow they weren't finished. At least, not according to Karen, who kept rehearsing the scene of their last meeting over and over in her mind. She could hear them argue and would think of things she wishes she'd said to convince Phyllis to apologize and prove her words to be untrue.

What's worse, Karen kept adding scenes to her mental double-feature. Now, in addition to picturing the scenario in which Phyllis had first betrayed her and then their unsatisfying meeting, she started adding more scenarios. In her head, Karen compiled a litany of all the times Phyllis had hurt her in the past. At the time, she had either ignored these or brushed them off as if they didn't bother her. But now, she could hear herself reciting each time she was hurt by Phyllis and thinking of cunning ways to get back at her, or at least to hate her.

Over the next few months, she would tell the people closest to her about the incident, and invariably she would get the support that she thought she wanted—which was "What? Phyllis said that! Oh, how awful! You are so right to be upset."

Finally, though, Karen's preoccupation with Phyllis was beginning to annoy even her. She started to realize she was wasting too much time and energy by giving Phyllis "rent-free" space in her head. In the theater of Karen's mind, at least, Phyllis got top billing and was the only show in town.

She said, "I'm keeping Phyllis in my life, front and center, but at the same time that she is no longer a part of it." She finally admitted, "I need to forgive."

Karen made another attempt to smooth things out with Phyllis. She asked her if they could sit down and talk, but was bluntly told: "No way! There's nothing more to talk about. You make mountains out of molehills. Get over it already!"

Phyllis's sharp tone of voice and cold-hearted attitude surprised Karen. "I couldn't believe she was the same person I knew all these years," Karen said.

Nothing has changed from their initial conversation after the fight until now. Phyllis won't budge to admit she was wrong. She accuses Karen of "exaggerating" everything.

After Karen shared the incident with me, she asked, "Why do I feel so out of sorts? I keep thinking, if only she would say 'I'm sorry,' I would forgive her in a heartbeat. But she isn't going to say 'sorry,' so I don't have a chance to say 'I forgive you.'"

Karen is close to forgiveness but she still needs a little fine-tuning to feel well again. So at the end of our session together, I gave her homework. I suggested she try the "Empty Chair Dialogue Technique" we learned in *Step 4: Rehearse* to begin healing and putting this episode behind her.

When she returned for her next session, Karen shared how the technique's imaginary conversation with Phyllis enabled her to express feelings she had been keeping to herself and had never had a chance to share. "I visualized Phyllis sitting across from me and I gave her a piece of my mind. I told her how disappointed and devastated I was with her gossiping with people she hardly knows. I shared all my hurtful feelings and then I stopped, switched places, and *listened to Phyllis*. I wanted desperately to understand what motivated her to do what she did and say what she did. But nothing changed. She maintained her innocence, saying she did nothing wrong."

It wasn't the answer Karen wanted to hear, but it did give her insights into Phyllis' lack of responsibility. She told me, "I believe Phyllis is too immature to say she's wrong and offer me an apology. Now, I have to get on with my life." She concluded, "I don't know if my friend and I will ever reconnect, but I'm feeling better by letting it go a little every day. I know I can't totally forgive until I am completely released of my anger and revenge. Since I've stopped focusing on Phyllis and started focusing on myself, I desire forgiveness. It's my flight to freedom. There are still days when I wake up to the old argument, but it doesn't have the same grip on my heart that it used to."

Without even knowing it, Karen has danced most of our steps to forgiveness: *Ruined* ("Phyllis gossiped behind my back and it hurts!"); *Retreat* ("I don't want anything to do with her; she'd better stay away…"); *Resent* ("I can't stand you!" "You'll pay for this…"); *Rehearse* ("I wish I had said this…" "Everybody agrees she's a -----"); *Rethink* ("This is driving me crazy, I have to let it go…"); *Respond* ("We need to sit down and talk…"); and *Reminder* ("I want her friendship, but I will not put up with…").

Now Karen needs to complete our eighth dance step, *Repair*, which intimately choreographs three movements: *yearn*, *learn*, and *turn*.

Yearn: Longing for the Way it Was

It's no secret, relationships break up; sometimes with a whimper, other times with a bang! Those that whimper simply dissolve from neglect, having run their natural course. Those that end with a bang are likely the result of an unexpected injury. Injuries can be so painful. The people we're intimately connected to know our darkest secrets. They have the power to hurt us precisely because they know us so well. If this happens, we have a choice: we can slam the door shut and keep it locked with anger and say, "I don't need her in my life" or "Why am I with him?" Or we can give ourselves space and time to cool off.

Learn: "I Don't Do That!"

At some point in our lives we "learn" that forgiveness means forgetting and approving of what happened to us. Nothing could be further from the truth. We need to "unlearn" this damaging lesson and relearn that forgiveness is neither forgetting nor approving. A close Methodist minister friend of mine took a stand of conscience that ultimately split his congregation. It was an extremely difficult and painful decision for him to make, but he felt that his integrity before God *required* that stand. When one of his supportive and active church members learned of his decision, he was extremely angry. He came to his office, and yelled at him in frustration. My friend tried his best to explain his position, but it didn't help him much. Before the gentleman stormed out, he said to the minister rather darkly, "I may forgive you for this, but I will never forget!"

Forgive and forget. Somehow, we think those two emotions go hand-in-hand. Here's what we need to learn: Forgetting may be the *result* of forgiveness but it's neither the means nor the test of forgiveness.

Let me draw that out a bit. Sometimes when we forgive a hurt, we'll truly forget it. I've had people come to apologize to me for something they did that I had long since forgotten, and couldn't even remember when they told me about it. Rejoice when we can do this: it's a gift to finally let go of the hurt so much that we actually have no conscious memory of the original slight.

But forgetting is *not* the means to forgiveness. We don't go about forgiving by trying to forget. In fact, the harder we try to forget something, the more deeply it will push that event down into our memory. It's like a person trying desperately to fall asleep—the harder they try, the more awake they become.

Forgetting is not the test of forgiveness. If we still remember a hurt, that doesn't necessarily mean that we haven't forgiven that person. The question is not whether we remember it, but what that memory does to us: whether our blood pressure goes up, our heart rate goes up, we feel bitterness in our hearts, or we act differently toward the offender.

There are times when we'll forgive those who hurt us even though we simply *cannot* forget. Forgiveness is not saying, "I don't feel the pain anymore." Forgiveness is saying to the person who hurt us, "I don't feel the need to hold onto your involvement in my pain anymore." Forgiveness is kicking that rent-free interloper out of your head, once and for all; it's shutting down the projector in that empty movie theater where you were the only one watching.

What has happened, happened. We must never deny that it was painful, that we were badly treated, and that we deplore the behavior that caused so much pain. Forgiveness has to do with learning not to be controlled by feelings of anger, bitterness, hatred, and revenge.

Likewise, we don't reduce our judgments about the seriousness of the injuries. We must not forget: our memories contribute to helping us guard against damaging experiences being repeated in the future. Ultimately, this is the challenge forgiveness presents us with: we need to hold onto the lesson learned without holding onto the pain. Forgiveness is choosing not to actively remember.

Forgiveness Is Not Approving

I listened quietly as Charlene told me the frank details of the sexual abuse she'd suffered as a child. "I hate my father!" she blurted out. "He abused me for more than a decade!" Charlene cried. "But," she explained, "my support group said if I want to heal from my childhood pain, I have to forgive."

"What did you tell your support group?" I asked.

"I told them I could never forgive my father, that I didn't want to forgive him, that no one—not even God—would expect me to forgive him! If I do, then I'm saying what he did was okay!" Charlene told me all the reasons that kept her from forgiving her abusive father. I'd heard many of them before. But despite her adamance, Charlene's thinking is a little incorrect. Forgiving her father's actions is in no way an approval of her father's abuse. What he did to her can never be condoned.

We were wrongly taught if we believe forgiveness means saying, "Oh, that's okay what you did to me." Forgiveness doesn't send the message that bad behavior is okay. Rather, it is saying that we're not going to continue to dwell on the past and carry the heavy feelings associated with it. When we lighten our emotional load, we refuse to allow the past to torment us in the present.

Approval doesn't come as a "side order" or "bonus offer" when we forgive. Forgiveness *doesn't* mean we approve of words said or actions done. We don't have to tolerate what someone has done to us in order to forgive them. In other words, we can forgive someone and still not approve of his or her behavior.

We can forgive and still refuse to accept what a person has done to us. We can let go of the past while holding onto what the experience has taught us. To forgive is to retain the wisdom while releasing the pain associated with the life lesson.

What Charlene's father did to her can never be accepted; nor is she likely ever to forget the experience. It's wrong, plain and simple. When we chose to forgive, we don't give cruel behavior the good housekeeping seal of approval.

Forgiveness, I've discovered, is a response that seeks to redeem the hurt, not brush it off. An accidental "slip of the tongue" needs no forgiveness because it isn't deliberately caused.

Intentional hurts—like Charlene's abuse—*need* forgiveness. When Charlene forgives her father, her forgiveness won't lessen the impact of his painful actions or diminish the memory. But forgiveness *will* unlock her own "prison" of anger, bitterness, and hatred so that she can move on with her life.

Turn: The Only Healthy Choice

The decision to patch up broken relationships by choosing forgiveness is the hardest choice we can ever make, but if we want to turn away from anger, hatred, and bitterness to peace, understanding, and compassion, we need to make it our healthy choice.

Some hurts seem too horrible to forgive. Our instincts tell us to avenge the person who caused us pain, not to release him or her from the debt owed us. But as Christians, we can't afford to have unforgiving hearts, for we have been greatly forgiven by God in Jesus Christ.

Only forgiveness can repair our relationships damaged from hurt. When we make the choice to patch up our relationships through forgiveness, we use our time and energy wisely so we can reconnect and grow closer together. Even if the offender doesn't want our forgiveness or fails to admit that he or she ever did anything wrong, there is still a relationship to salvage through forgiveness—and that is the precious relationship we have with ourselves!

When we forgive, we stop building walls, striking back, starting rumors, gaining support, or dismissing people from our lives completely. Instead, we listen closely, trying to get inside the other person's world and see what happened through his or her eyes. We make it a safe place for each of us to openly express our feelings. And we commit to practice constructive behavior in our relationships, rather than continue in the destructive behavior of jealousy, pettiness, or spite. We promise to make things as right as possible through forgiveness.

Once we forgive and we're reconnected, our relationships suddenly have boundaries. These are not the walls of the prison of unforgiveness we've been living in but rather "gates" that allow us to let in what is good and keep out what is bad.

Forgiving is sometimes a complicated and long dance, complete with stubbed toes and aching calves. We may need some time to rest our feet before our relationships are completely repaired, but the nice thing is that this is all "on the job" training; we are repairing them as we dance. Because we yearn to have people in our lives, we work harder to resolve our hurts, repair our relationships, and restore our love.

When we say, "I forgive you" or "I'm sorry," we say goodbye to anger, bitterness, hatred, and revenge. We stop living in the land of "if only" and start accepting "what is" so we can move forward on life's path to enjoy "what's next." In unforgiveness we are broken, half-alive, and incomplete. We turn to forgiveness to be whole again.

Something to Consider (Ponder)

Donnie said to his fishing buddy Charlie, "When me and the wife fight, she gets historical."

"Historical?" Charlie asks.

"Yes, historical," replies Donnie.

"You mean hysterical, don't you?" asks Charlie.

"No, historical. She remembers everything I have ever said or done, brings it up, and throws it right in my face. She forgets nothing."

Do you have someone in your life like Donnie's wife?

How do you deal with a person who keeps resurrecting the past, someone who keeps getting historical instead of hysterical?

Think about this: Many people are afraid to forgive because they feel they must remember the wrong. Through forgiveness, the wrong is released from its emotional stranglehold on us so that we can learn from it. Can such a person ever bury the hatchet, without remembering where it is buried?

Something to Do (Practice)

Only one mourner showed up at the chapel that day—the seventy-six-year-old daughter of the deceased.

> *"If we really want to love, we must learn how to forgive."*
>
> MOTHER TERESA

"Tell me about your father," I said. "He must have been a positive man to have lived to be 102."

"Not really," she confessed. "He didn't know how to forgive people and love them. His famous line was, 'You only get one bite out of the apple and then you're finished.' For my father, it was 'one and done.' I don't think I ever heard him say, 'I'm sorry' or 'I accept your apology.' His circle of friends and associates dwindled over the years because he couldn't forgive and love. He just wrote them off. I'm crying for what could have been if he had been able to let go, give people another chance, and learn to care."

As we walked toward the chapel door, she stopped, placed her hand on the casket and said, "Too late!"

Too late! If you're living with a broken and disconnected relationship, don't wait until tomorrow to take care of it, to patch the roof or "spackle" the ceiling. Make an effort to take care of it today. Don't leave the apologies left unsaid and the forgiveness withheld.

Something to Say (Prayer)

Forgiving God, there are times when I allow hurtful people to run my life. They may have ruined my yesterdays, but only I am in charge of my tomorrows.

I once cherished and valued my relationships, and it's time for me to step up to the plate and patch up the broken ones. I know it will take patience and persistence, since I have consistently ignored apologies offered and have stubbornly chosen to push people out of my life. I am going to start today to bring down the walls and mend the fences through the dance to forgiveness. I now believe forgiveness has the power to change my anger and desire for wanting a pound of flesh into understanding, compassion, and loving kindness.

Loving God, I know my relationships will never be as they were before the hurt. But I know they can become stronger and healthier, once everything is out in the open. I am going to speak the truth about what happened, the anger I felt, and the things I need to say. Then I'm going to close my mouth and let them speak. And when everything is said that needs to be said, I will forgive.

I will bury the hatchet completely and forget where it is buried. In Jesus' name, I pray. Amen.

❧ STEP 9 ❧

Reward

Reaping Benefits

"But love your enemies, and do good, and lend, expecting nothing in return; and your reward will be great." ❧ LUKE 6:35

Who hasn't felt the sting of betrayal, unfair treatment, or something more abusive? Many of us cling to the resulting rage and hurt, but others choose to forgive. Are they superhumans, robots, or automatons? Are they different from you and me? Hardly. They are simply people who realized, sooner than most, that the pain they were inflicting was all internal; that it was time to move on and that forgiveness was the road map to the future.

When we forgive, we completely release ourselves from all hurts. Forgiveness enables us to overcome anger, bitterness, and hatred, together with a desire to punish or get even with someone who injured us. It's important to remember, however excruciating the hurt, it will be eclipsed by the joy of meaningful forgiveness.

The dance is worth it.

Something to Learn (Path)

I talked with Randy, who divorced his wife, Cindy, after twenty years of marriage. After talking for fifty minutes, he declared, "I will never forgive her" for this; "I will never forgive her" for that. I can understand his frustration. However, I don't understand what he's trying to accomplish by saying, "I will never forgive her."

Cindy's affairs, lies, and cover-ups just got to be too much for Randy. He told me he lives by the old saying, "Burn me once, shame on you. Burn me twice, shame on me." He said, "Anyone can be taken in once, but if I make myself vulnerable a second time, I'm the fool. Well, I am a fool, a big one. I believed lie after lie and now I'm full of multiple burns."

Divorced now for two years, Randy is still fuming. "Every time I see her, my blood boils, my heart pounds, and I get so tense that I literally feel sick." I finally asked him, "Do you really think you're punishing Cindy by not forgiving her?" Surprisingly, his response was, "I know I'm not punishing her because she's cold and clueless. I just hate her for what she did to me."

Randy hasn't come to an awareness that he's not hurting Cindy, but only himself. He needs to enroll quickly in the "Forgiveness School of Dance" and start dancing the steps before he turns himself into a miserable old man that people don't want to be around.

We have arrived at our ninth dance step, *Reward*. It's time for us to reap the benefits forgiveness pours into our lives—or bear the burdens, if we're going to dig in our heels and refuse to forgive, like Randy.

Despite its benefits, Randy will not even consider forgiveness as an option. That's a big mistake. Hanging onto a hurt for years means making a commitment to remaining angry. That means while Cindy moves on with her life, Randy will be treading water right where he is: deep in the sea of unforgiveness.

An Apology a Day

Forgiveness is important, not just because I say so but because it manages anger, cuts stress, and, most importantly, improves health. When we're unable to forgive someone who has hurt us, we remain linked to that person, and it wears us down and causes us health concerns.

If left unchecked, these concerns can turn into serious health issues. Anyone who has had a few sleepless nights, who has felt stressed out at work for a week, sweating out that new account, or waited twenty minutes to hear bad news in the doctor's office can tell you how disrupting such concerns can be. Now stretch those short-term stress incidents into weeks, months, and even years, and you'll begin to see the deleterious effect unforgiveness can have.

More and more medical doctors, social scientists, and spiritual writers are extolling the proven health benefits of forgiveness. Forgiveness can result in less anxiety and depression, better health outcomes, increased coping with stress, and increased closeness to God and others.

Evidence is mounting that harboring negative emotions like blame, anger, and hostility (the ones we feel the most when we're nursing a grudge) can damage our cardiovascular, nervous, and immune systems. Other studies are uncovering evidence that practicing forgiveness (essentially, releasing those poisonous feelings) can improve physical health in significant ways, too, offering numerous healthy benefits in the bargain.

Here's a litany of healthy benefits available when we dance to forgiveness: healing of emotional and physical pain; lower heart rate and blood pressure; reduced stress; more physical and mental energy; better quality sleep; better daily attitude; longer life; increased happiness and peace of mind; being friendlier and more tolerant; decreased depression; more positive outlook on life; less anger and hostility; fewer "pieces" of emotional baggage; faster reaction time; getting a new life!

The choice is ours. Forgiveness opens up a new world of health, as well as positive and emotional freedom. On the other hand, if we choose to cling to our hurt, we can expect to jeopardize our health in return. The body manufactures "high voltage" chemicals like adrenaline and cortisone when we hold anger and resentment. As a result, our minds remain in a constant state of "flight or fight."

These toxic chemicals will result in tension-related ills such as headaches, high blood pressure, and abdominal pains. Left unchecked, we'll experience more serious problems from these lingering emotional toxins, such as chronic pain, ulcers, sluggishness, gastritis, irritable bowel syndrome, chronic fatigue, and, in the worst case scenario, cancer. Forgiveness has profound healthy benefits, while purging our anger may also help heal some of what ails us physically.

Marie's revelation about these amazing health benefits came at a chance meeting with her estranged friend. "Instead of turning away like I usually would," she said, "I told her how deeply she had hurt me. She listened, but didn't apologize. Then I surprised myself. I apologized! I apologized for harboring anger and hatred against her for so long. As I spoke, I realized I had just forgiven her."

The effect was potent—and prompt. "My anger suddenly melted away," she says, the emotional and physical relief was clearly evident on her face. Marie hasn't renewed the friendship, unfortunately, but now when she sees her ex-friend, "I can breathe calmly and my heart isn't palpitating."

Continuously dancing to forgiveness gives us back our emotional freedom and happiness. We can finally say "good riddance" to depression, anger, bitterness, hatred, paybacks, tension, impatience, irritability, and negativity. Forgiveness makes us wiser and stronger. It makes us easier to love, and it makes life itself just plain easier.

Cleansing Our Souls

Our soul is the safe harbor where we go to hear God's encouraging and healing voice speak to us during the difficult and joyful times of life. It's so important to cleanse our souls by stripping away all the layers of unhealthy emotions that have accumulated over the years. Much the same way a dirty windshield obstructs our view of a busy street full of playing children, all these layers of toxic emotions block us from hearing God speak to us.

Anger, hatred, obsessive thoughts about the hurt, or calculating a plan to "get even" entangle us and hinder us. This is not the real us; this is now our normal "default" setting. Our souls become congested with all this emotional sludge, but our unforgiveness requires that we keep the sludge around "just in case." Instead of running our God-appointed race with joy, we sentence ourselves to an emotional cesspool of our own design.

Got Soul Sludge?

Soul cleansing is similar to computer usage. When we use a computer and constantly add large files, the hard drive gets clogged up. Performance slows. To clean it up, we close all running programs, delete all unnecessary temporary and duplicate files, run an error checker program, and even defragment the hard drive to consolidate the isolated clusters of the drive.

When we don't cleanse our souls of anger, bitterness, hatred, and revenge, our souls become clogged like that computer— a jam-packed warehouse where fresh ideas, caring voices, and quality living can't pass through the sludge.

Forgiveness cleanses our soul, thus giving us the wisdom to discern and decide which battles we're going to fight. We can then claim the power to run our own lives and not be ruled by our past hurts. I've discovered one powerful remedy that can strip away all those layers of anger, bitterness, and hatred—heavy doses of prayer.

Take Jesus seriously when he teaches the importance of prayer, of going into our rooms, closing the door and talking with God. We have to find a quiet place where we can sit while we rendezvous with God: a corner at home, a favorite seat in church, or a park bench will work. Just as having one particular booth to meet friends at a restaurant is special, having one place to meet Jesus in prayer becomes a gift to our souls.

Then spill; let it all out! Let's allow God to take us through the emotional geography we might otherwise avoid. Ask God to help us explore the uncomfortable, especially those hurtful feelings we tend to stuff inside. Don't worry; God doesn't take off points for awkward pauses, poor grammatical construction, or unexpected emotional outbursts.

Praying knits our hearts together with God's heart. Pray often. Then embrace the quiet and listen to God's gentle voice. A comforting voice: "I understand you're hurting." "It wasn't right what happened to you." A challenging voice: "Let go of all the bad stuff before it destroys you." "Go and repair the relationship before it's too late." A caring voice: "I'm with you, no matter what happens." "Forgive. Forgive. And forgive again."

There is nothing quite as beneficial as the full feeling of forgiveness—both when that forgiveness is received and also when it is shared. Let's not carry any of the old junk around with us any longer. Let's free up space on our internal hard drive and keep those feet dancing toward forgiveness so we can finally let the past fade away and be gone, once and for all.

Lest you think forgiveness is a new phenomenon, remember this: Jesus was *very* serious about forgiveness. He said we will be forgiven with the same measure we forgive. Paul urged us to accept that we've been hurt, to put aside all desires of getting even, and be kind, gentle, tenderhearted, and forgiving, as God in Jesus has forgiven us. When God forgives, it's done and will never come up again.

Something to Consider (Ponder)

Have you ever been cheated on or mistreated? Got any lingering grudges you're holding onto? Is there any "unclear air" between you and a family member, neighbor, or coworker regarding a dispute, a slight, an offense? Has a neighbor defamed or dissed you? Has a family member consistently called your reputation into account? Could those situations use some forgiveness?

Daily life brings many sources of conflict to *all of us*. Injuries can lead to resentment and bitterness, then anger, explosion, and even violence. There are many opportunities in life to become angry with another person because of "a look" or a thoughtless act, or an unkind word, or a "stupid" idea. This anger can shut down communication and prevent us from working together. It can short-circuit our good sense and cause us to close ourselves off from healthy, beneficial relationships; it can cause us to make bad decisions *now* that affect our very future.

Watch the movie *12 Angry Men* (1957) and record the times when a look, an act, a word, or an idea could have created a problem. Now consider the following questions: Did others respond to this "wrongdoing" with forgiveness or anger? Where did anger take them? What would a forgiving response have looked like or sounded like? What burdens are carried from not forgiving? What benefits are reaped from forgiving?

When we add forgiveness to our dance routine, healing, reconciliation, and restoration can follow, and the benefits keep rolling in.

Something to Do (Practice)

Shortly before his death, C.S. Lewis wrote, "I think I have at last forgiven the cruel schoolmaster who so darkened my youth. I had done it many times before, but this time I think I have really done it." Does this sound like something we would say?

Make copies of the following wonderful poem and give it to those who are reluctant (or too stubborn) to get on the dance floor to forgiveness. Share with them the benefits from being able to say, "I forgive you."

Forgiveness

Author Unknown

> *To forgive*
>> *Is not to forget*
>
> *To forgive*
>> *Is really to remember*
>> *That nobody is perfect*
>> *That each of us stumbles*
>> *When we want so much to stay upright*
>> *That each of us says things*
>> *We wish we had never said*
>> *That we can all forget that love*
>> *Is more important than being right.*
>
> *To forgive*
>> *Is really to remember*
>> *That we are so much more*
>> *Than our mistakes*
>> *That we are often more kind and caring*
>> *That accepting another's flaws*
>> *Can help us accept our own.*
>
> *To forgive*
>> *Is to remember*

That the odds are pretty
good that
We might soon need to
be forgiven ourselves
That life sometimes gives
us more
Than we can handle
gracefully.

To forgive
Is to remember
That we have room in
our hearts to
Begin again
And again
And again.

Ready to clear up your hard-drive of all those unhealthy, negative emotions? Good. Now write down a list of negative and unhealthy emotions you want to clean out of your soul. Next to each emotion, write how you'll sweep it out of your life. For example, if fear of saying "I'm sorry" clogs your soul, choose to pause, catch a breath, remain calm, and then act in spite of the fear.

> *"A Christian will find it cheaper to pardon than to resent. Forgiveness saves the expense of anger, the cost of hatred, and the waste of spirit."*
>
> HANNAH MORE

Something to Say (Prayer)

Generous God, thank you for forgiving me over and over again. I'm trying myself to burn all the score cards I have been keeping on those who have hurt me and I'm trying my best to tell myself "to be quiet" when a painful memory pops into my head. I want to turn them over to you in prayer and leave them with you.

When I forgive, the benefits far outweigh the burdens. I feel like a tremendous load has been lifted off my shoulder. I'm happy with who I am: compassionate, accepting, understanding, and loving. I'm not snapping at people, but accepting them where they are.

I have learned, dear God, that forgiveness is me giving up my right to hurt anyone for hurting me. In Jesus' name, I pray. Amen.

STEP 10

Release
Moving On

"Which is easier, to say, 'Your sins are forgiven,' or to say, 'Get up, and walk'?"   MATTHEW 9:5

Moving on is something we do when we are stuck in a dead end. How long have we been there, circling the drain? Days? Weeks? Months? Years?!? How long we've been there matters far less than how long we're willing to stay. Dance Step 10, *Release*, finds us moving on from the dead end of unforgiveness toward a brighter future of forgiveness, healing, and hope.

Something to Learn (Path)

Not too long ago someone encouraged me to read Exodus 14:15. I did, and now these words have become my compass for navigating through life's hurdles, hassles, and heartaches, but especially when someone hurts me. The Lord's words to Moses inspired me to stay on my feet and keep dancing to forgiveness. The verse says, "Why are you crying out to me? Tell the Israelites to move on."

I love that. Sometimes we really do just need to *move on*.

Need to apologize to someone? Apologize. Move on. Need to forgive someone? Forgive. Move on. Are there "issues" and baggage to drop before we can make a clean getaway from unforgiveness? Let go of the baggage, with professional help if necessary. Just move on. In a go-nowhere relationship? Either give it all you've got to repair it, or declare it officially dead.

Once we forgive, it may take time to be healed completely. For some, it may take weeks; for others, it may take years. The point is not comparing how long it takes but in recognizing that we have made the first official step to forgiveness. We have to stay on the dance floor until the day we no longer feel anger over the injury.

The time it takes to completely forgive a person doesn't matter. It's the time we begin forgiving that changes our lives. While doing that, we're also allowing ourselves to release the hurt that otherwise will be kept inside for as long as we choose not to forgive. Inherently, moving on means leaving something behind; in this case, we are leaving the grudge that has done us no favors in this life.

Release Your 4Gs

Step 10 *Release* completes our repertoire of dance steps to forgiveness by encouraging us to keep moving on. We can't stand still forever; eventually we have to take a step toward healing the hurts of the past. This begins with healing ourselves first. Specifically, forgiveness releases us from the 4Gs of unforgiveness: Gotcha People, the Gnawing Pain, the Get-Even Plans, and the God-Awful Pain.

Gotcha People

Even though people we care about have hurt us, maybe even gotten the best of us, we either come back together in our relationships or we abandon them completely. Even when we're angry with people, we can still care deeply about our relationships with them. Unforgiving people are usually quick to abandon a relationship; to start talking about divorce, to start thinking the person isn't worth having as a friend, to seriously consider disowning a son or daughter. They dance alone and don't know the steps of the dance to forgiveness.

Forgiving people bring their hurt out to the surface. Once admitting it and owning it, the dance to forgiveness can continue. Then we dance to patch up the relationship by talking and listening and establishing boundaries so the hurtful behavior will not be repeated.

Gnawing Past

The roots of our hurts are like a gnarled old tree stump that's buried deep down inside. No wonder it hurts! Forgiveness unties the tangled mess and eventually helps us let go of the anger, bitterness, and hatred that cause hurt and distress. It's the state we reach when what happened in the past is emotionally in the past.

Forgiving has to do with editing our own memory. We don't completely erase what has happened, but our past wounds are healed so our present isn't affected by them. We know that it happened and how it affected us, but our current lives aren't determined by that experience. By being released from our past, it doesn't become a regret of the present, gnawing at our potential until we, too, feel hopeless and "hungry" for more.

We can't separate the person from the hurt. But we can release the person from our memory of the hurt we experienced. As long as we remain fastened to the past, we let our anger, bitterness, and hate control our dance steps. Forgiving is allowing a new dance step to develop. We don't pretend that we didn't suffer, but we don't let it determine what happens right now either.

Get-Even Plans

When we get rid of this third G, we stop running various scenarios through our minds fantasizing about payback. Our logbooks, scorecards, or mental files of injuries done to us are shredded, burned, or deleted. We quit trying to be directors of our own "revenge flick" where we're the good guy, hunting down the bad emotions one by one until none are left. By letting go of the need to hurt back and be able to move on with our lives, we unlock the door to our own prison and step out into freedom.

God-Awful Pain

Through the marvelous dance of forgiveness, we find a way to free ourselves of the burden of chronic anger, bitterness, and hatred, no matter how badly we've been hurt.

Andy said, "I was tired of having my life ruled by anger and hatred. I was an active member on the 'Plotting and Planning Committee' with other men or women seeking revenge on the person who hurt them. It didn't help soothe my hurt; it was making me settle for being a person I wasn't happy becoming. I decided I needed to get this resolved. It took me months to work through the feelings, but I did, and I have forgiven Teresa for what she did."

Ultimately, who wants to have a life defined by unhealthy feelings? Forgiving the person who hurt us can't be forced (or rushed, for that matter), but if we're open to the possibility, it *will* come at the right time and the right place.

Andy told me he woke up one morning and thought, "Now is the time to move on and put this behind me." He said, "We're no longer together, but we can now talk respectfully and act maturely around our family and friends."

Got Soul?

Have you ever watched *Everybody Loves Raymond*? One of the most popular TV sitcoms of the past decade, this beloved sitcom was built around the brilliant work of Ray Romano, a former stand-up comic who successfully made the transition from comedian to TV star. Romano became one of the most successful and highly paid personalities in his industry. When the final episode of the show ended in 2005, Romano walked out on the set and spoke to the studio audience. He told them about a note his older brother Richard had stuck in his luggage when he moved from New York to Hollywood nine years earlier. Richard wrote, "What does it profit a man if he gains the whole world and loses his soul?"

"Now," said a tearful Romano to a live audience, "I'm going to work on my soul."

I hope it is going well for him.

I often hear people say things like

"Why should I forgive my father? His addiction destroyed my mother and ruined our home life."

"Why should I forgive the person who raped me? He made it so I'll never really trust a man again."

"Why should I forgive my friend? He or she violated my trust."

"Why should I forgive her? She ran my name through the mud with no concern at all!"

"Why should I forgive my spouse for cheating on me? I'll never get those ten years back!"

"Why should I forgive my parents for divorcing? They ruined my childhood."

Clearly, the answers to these questions have little to do with human fairness, which demands an eye for an eye, or with excusing, which means brushing it off. The ultimate answer, of course, has *everything* to do with forgiveness.

Guilty of "Soul Neglect"?

At first, we feel our hearts pounding, our stomachs churning, and our thoughts racing in dark directions. Keep nursing this feeling and we're headed straight for soul neglect. What is soul neglect? It's when we take our soul for granted, when we neglect the source of happiness and hope that resides within each of us in favor of savoring long-term thoughts of vengeance, retaliation, and unforgiveness.

Jesus had it right all along. He warns us, "It's what comes out of us that pollutes us" (Matthew 15:11). Clinging to anger and resentment plagues our souls. Our souls become lost when covered with layers of unhealthy feelings. We become so consumed with this other person that we lose touch with who we are and being who we want to be. We're so obsessed with dwelling in the past that we miss connecting in healthy relationships and healing our hurts in the present.

Forgiveness is the balm that soothes our souls and lets us focus on what's important to us. I've seen it and experienced it personally: once we're able to let go of hurts that have been done to us, *it changes everything*. It will change our relationships, our attitudes, our emotional make-up—inside and out—our whole approach to living. It will give us a better life.

Forgiveness sets up a reunion between who you used to be and who you are now. Have you ever watched the show *Intervention*? Each episode follows a seemingly hopeless addict through turbulence and tumult, heading toward rock bottom, and eventually an intervention. Some folks take the gift offered in the intervention, for example, a stay in rehab, while others refuse it outright. Some folks go to rehab but quit early or are kicked out. My favorite episodes are the ones where someone goes to rehab and lets it work; when someone goes through the process and rediscovers himself or herself.

Often they'll disavow who they were on drugs, looking at old pictures or even video footage and saying, "I don't remember that," or "I can't believe that was me," or "I can't believe I went down that far." Post-rehab they often look radiant and have a positive, hopeful attitude.

That is what forgiveness does too; it erases that "middle part" where so much damage was done, and it lets us reconnect with who we were before this event turned us into someone vengeful and unfamiliar. Do you remember that person? Don't you want to reunite with him or her? What's stopping you?

Our dance steps encourage us to shed the bitterness and drop the revenge. They lead to saying, "I forgive you." It's only then we're released to embrace others again; it's only then that we can reunite with our former selves and begin anew.

Something to Consider (Ponder)

Watch the movie *Dead Man Walking* (1995). It tells the true story of how an unsuspecting Catholic nun became the spiritual director of a death row inmate, Matthew Poncelet, who is awaiting his execution by lethal injection for the brutal murder of a teenage couple.

Throughout the movie, Matthew does little to help us identify with him as a human being. He's sickening and repulsive. Yet Sister Prejean continues to guide him, hoping somehow to touch his soul. Finally, she leads him to an act of contrition and penance. As a result, he declares to the parents of his victims, "I hope that my death gives you some peace."

But for the parents of the young girl, there is no peace. The only thing they have is hate. And under the circumstance, their reaction is understandable, even natural. But, the father of the

> *"You are searching for the one key that will unlock the door to the source of forgiveness; and yet you have the key in your own hands; use it."*
>
> UNKNOWN

young man is not as hardened. He attends the graveside services for the murderer, but stands at a distance.

Sister Prejean goes to him and he tells her, "Sister, I wish I had your faith."

She replies, "It's not faith. It's a lot of WORK."

And how right she is; forgiveness *is* hard. We, too, have to work at it.

In his letter to the Philippians, Paul writes, "I do not count myself to have apprehended; but one thing I do, forgetting those things which are behind and reaching forward to those things which are ahead, I press toward the goal for the prize of the upward call of God in Christ Jesus" (Philippians 3:14–15).

To seek the ultimate in forgiveness, Paul had to forget his past achievements (as an esteemed Jewish leader). He also had to forget his past failures (which including persecuting and killing Christians).

What hurts are we carrying today that we should have set down a long time ago?

Something to Do (Practice)

Purchase an old fashioned skeleton key. You can find them in antique stores or thrift shops all around the country. Keep it in your pocket, purse, briefcase, car, or on your desk. Wear it around your neck if you like.

Why? It can be a reminder that we've been released from the prison of unforgiveness. We're set free and the only thing we need to do now is put one foot in front of the other and keep moving on and embracing all that life has to offer.

Better yet, buy two skeleton keys. If you have been fortunate enough to watch a friend, parent, spouse, or child dance through the steps of forgiveness, give him or her one as a sign that they, too, are released and set free.

Something to Say (Prayer)

Compassionate God, forgiveness is always going be a challenging dance, but I'm ready to put on my dancing shoes. Give me the wisdom to step back often and enter this place of prayer where I can be alone with you and reinforce my desire to stay on the forgiveness dance floor. Remind me that my relationships are more important that my own hurt and pride and though the dance is not easy, the end result will set me free.

God, you have invited me to join in this dance of forgiveness. I don't have to remain standing outside in my anger and hurt. You are with me always, so I will do my best to forgive over and over again. I know this for sure: Life is too short and too precious to waste. In Jesus' name, I pray. Amen.

Let's Make Up

I stopped briefly to watch two children quarreling. Their dialogue went something like this:

"You're stupid!"

"Well, so are you."

"Not as stupid as you!"

"Oh, yeah? That's what *you* think."

They soon finished their exchange and went their separate ways. When I returned not more than ten minutes later, the children were playing again, getting along peacefully, having clearly forgotten the whole thing. No brooding, no wounded egos, no blame, no dredging up the past, and no plan for revenge. A brief exchange, an even briefer cooling-off period, and all is forgotten. Such is the world of children.

For grown-ups, of course, forgiveness is not a quick, one-sided, kiss-and-make-up response. Adults develop razor-sharp memories of past wrongs and carry them around, ready at a moment's notice to use them as ammunition. The days of playground breakups and make-ups have long given way to grievances, grudges, and unforgiveness.

Picking Your Tune

Every time we think of something in our past that has caused us great pain, we must choose the musical tune for our dance to forgiveness. It's a simple choice, really. In fact, there are only two songs on the playlist: *Carry It Circle* or *Bury It Boulevard*.

Yet Jesus wants to set us free so we can get on with our lives. He can and does relate to our hurts. He knows that some of the hardest blows in life come from the people we love. He was laughed at, mocked, beaten up, and deserted by friends. Jesus knows all about being hurt. It is to our great advantage to welcome him into our hurts. He has the most experience with forgiveness, so we can share his wisdom and let him influence our decisions. When Jesus comes, we don't have to clean up our mess first. He doesn't say, "Get your act together and *then* come to me." He says, "Let me into your mess and I'll help you heal it. I'm gentle and humble and kindhearted."

Jesus will give us the strength to pick ourselves up, and patch up our relationships so we can find the happiness that we seek.

For years I have saved an article written by the scholar and Holocaust survivor Elie Wiesel. In it, Wiesel expresses the most profound act of forgiveness imaginable. It's here that he actually expresses forgiveness toward God for the Holocaust. Wiesel asks God the question he has struggled with all his life: "Where were you, God of Kindness, in Auschwitz?" He had never been able to understand how a loving God could have allowed the Holocaust to exist. But out of the question that has tormented him for fifty years, he gleans a sudden insight: "Watching your children suffer at the hands of your other children, haven't you also suffered?"

In this moment of wanting to be released from the feelings he has carried about God, Wiesel is finally moved to offer God his forgiveness: "Let us make up, Master of the Universe," he says. "In spite of everything that happened? Yes, in spite. Let us make up: for the child in me, it's unbearable to be divorced from you for so long."

Elie Wiesel could easily be our dance partner when we vow never to forgive an insult received in anger, a trust broken by betrayal, a slight delivered out of forgetfulness, a secret revealed by gossip, a reputation tainted by rumors, or a hurt born out of a misunderstanding. However, holding on to anger and hurt only enslaves us. Releasing these emotions through forgiveness frees us to move forward more happily.

Elie Wiesel's story is a reminder to us all that only forgiveness releases us from the emotional hurts caused by others, enabling us to keep moving on and growing as persons. For the child in all of us, we must dance to forgiveness. And for the sake of the children we love with unparalleled intensity, we must model the most noble and humbling of all dances, the dance of forgiveness.

"And when you get the choice to sit it out or dance, I hope you dance, I hope you dance."

LEE ANN WOMACK